*an application of*
# PSYCHOANALYSIS *to* EDUCATION

*Publication Number 384*

AMERICAN LECTURE SERIES®


*A Monograph in*

AMERICAN LECTURES IN PSYCHOLOGY


*Edited by*

MOLLY HARROWER, Ph.D.

*Professor of Research in Clinical Psychology*
*in the*
*Department of Psychiatry*
*Temple University School of Medicine*
*Philadelphia, Pennsylvania*

# *an application of*
# ‖ PSYCHOANALYSIS *to* EDUCATION

*By*

**RICHARD M. JONES, Ph. D.**

*Department of Psychology*
*Brandeis University*
*Waltham, Massachusetts*


*With an Introduction by*

**LAWRENCE S. KUBIE, M. D.**

*Director of Training, The Sheppard and Enoch Pratt Hospital*
*Towson, Maryland*
*Clinical Professor of Psychiatry*
*Yale University School of Medicine (on leave)*
*Faculty, New York Psychoanalytic Institute (on leave)*
*Lecturer in Psychiatry*
*College of Physicians and Surgeons*
*Columbia University*
*New York City*

CHARLES C THOMAS • PUBLISHER

*Springfield • Illinois • U. S. A.*

CHARLES C THOMAS · PUBLISHER
BANNERSTONE HOUSE
301-327 East Lawrence Avenue, Springfield, Illinois, U.S.A.


*Published simultaneously in the British Commonwealth of Nations by*
BLACKWELL SCIENTIFIC PUBLICATIONS, LTD., OXFORD, ENGLAND


*Published simultaneously in Canada by*
THE RYERSON PRESS, TORONTO

With THOMAS BOOKS careful attention is given to all details of
manufacturing and design. It is the Publisher's desire to present books
that are satisfactory as to their physical qualities and artistic possibilities
and appropriate for their particular use. THOMAS BOOKS will be true
to those laws of quality that assure a good name and good will.

*Printed in the United States of America*

*To Audrey*

# INTRODUCTION

THROUGHOUT our educational system a realization is growing that both intellectual development and creativity will continue to be seriously hampered unless we find out how to make emotional maturation a part of education. Consequently educators are preoccupied increasingly with the difficult problems attendant on the attempt to introduce self-knowledge-in-depth into the main stream of formal education. They recognize that if this is to be done at all, it must start in the kindergarten and continue throughout the elementary grades, grammar school, high school, college and graduate years.

"Progressive education" was one of the early efforts in this direction. Originally, however, this involved a misapplication to education processes of techniques which are sometimes essential in formal psychotherapy. The predictable failures of these well-meant but inept efforts caused the climate of education to swing back temporarily to an opposite extreme, i.e., back to the old-fashioned techniques of drill and grill, and more drill and more grill.

A newer realization of the full complexity of these problems is now developing: i.e., that there is an incessant interaction between universal but subtly masked neurotic mechanisms and the educational process, and that as a result of this interplay education is blocked and distorted. The relationship between the two is evidently so close, that both must be solved if either is to be solved.

This does not, however, force us to the impossible conclusion that every teacher must be an analytically trained psychotherapist or that every school child must be psychoanalyzed. It brings us rather to conclude that all education should be conducted in an atmosphere in which the universal and recurrent emotional disturbances and repressive tendencies of childhood can be resolved as soon as they arise, and before they become chronic. The child's fifth freedom is the right to know what he feels; but this does not carry with it any right to act out his feelings blindly. This will require a new mores for our schools, one which will enable young people from early years to understand and feel and put into words all the hidden things which go on inside of them, thus ending the conspiracy of silence with which the development of the child is now distorted both at home and at school. If the conspiracy of silence is to be replaced by the fifth freedom, children must be encouraged and helped to attend to their forbidden thoughts, and to put them into words, i.e., to talk out loud about love and hate and jealousy and fear, about curiosity over the body, its products and its apertures; about what goes in and what comes out; about what happens inside and what happens outside; about their dim and confused feelings about sex itself; about the strained and stressful relationships within families, which are transplanted into schools. All of these are things about which school must help children to become articulate in the schoolroom.

Once any child becomes free in this sense then his great preconscious creative capacity will be freed from the retarding weight of pedestrian, literal, conscious processes, and at the same time from the distortions which arise out of neurotogenic and psychotogenic unconscious processes.

The work which Dr. Richard M. Jones describes in this volume is an experiment which is unique in many respects. Its goal is to lift the conspiracy of silence. Therefore it is a path-finding experiment, a careful study of which will be rewarding to all who wish to pursue investigations in this direction. It is a welcome innovation in the field of education to find a synthesis of clean-cut experimental design, clear psychological and psychoanalytic thinking, and cautious concern for the welfare of the youngsters who are the voluntary subjects of the experiment.

LAWRENCE S. KUBIE, M.D.

# PREFACE

IT HAS BEEN heartening to note the recent ironic outgrowth of the armaments race into a simultaneous educations race. Enthusiasm at this turn in world events should, I believe, be tempered only by the observation that on the western side the militance of our sudden upswelling regard for the care of children's intellects is in danger of doing modern experimental education in just at the moment when it was taking a second wind. True, the increasing number of celestial reminders that we fool around with basic education at our possible peril will curtail the frightening intrusion into traditional curricula of psychologized courses in well-adjusted be-goodism and psycho-evangelistic togetherness. The bastardizations of Dewey's earlier and well-taken reforms, however, would have dwindled from their own endogenous impoverishment—having had no roots, really, in any authentic philosophy or psychology. The more the pity, then, that there speedy demise may now come at the hands of crash program reactionists, with the risk of hindering educational theorists and researchers in the task of re-orienting "progressive" education from its frayed ties with nineteenth century rationalist psychologies to a liaison with psychoanalytic psychology. The present study may be viewed as counter-reactionary in this regard.

Another spotlighted issue of the times with which we find ourselves grappling in this study is that of reducing race prejudice. I wish to note at the outset, therefore, that the study was conceived and concluded not only before the Sputnik made a controversy of what should be going on in classrooms, but also before the Supreme Court made a controversy of *with whom*. The reader with an appetite for what Gordon Allport used to call "the simple and sovereign solution" may thus be deterred from so eyeing this monograph in respect to either controversy.

Rather, will he find here a piece of "action research," a conception first used by Kurt Lewin (62) and defined by Jerome Bruner (20) as: ". . . studies which, while seeking to achieve a socially useful end, are also devoted to the systematic collection of data and the testing of hypotheses."

The "action" half of the study sought to fill a gap that in recent years has become an object of concern in the field of education. The "research" half of the study sought to fill a gap created but as yet unbridged by the many investigations of ethnic prejudice that have been prominent in social psychological journals over the past decade and a half.

Part I, then, includes the description and evaluation of an educational method for deepening attitudes of self tolerance, and Part II includes the testing of hypotheses pertaining to concomitant changes in attitudes of ethnic tolerance. Since the setting of the study, its design, and procedure carry overlapping pertinence to both parts, these will be described first.

Much credit for the study goes to Mrs. Alnah Johnston, who knows a bargain when she sees one—and knows how to keep it. Leo Berman's work at the junctures of psychoanalysis and education was a source of steady guidance. Royce Pitkin and his crew of practical idealists at Goddard College, who for the past five years have made their Vermont hills and gardens— and conference room —an annual retreat for the mutual re-dedication of lonely educators-in-depth, must also accept a place as my intellectual creditors. Finally, in back of the study stood three giants; each, in his own way, and educator *of* educators-in-depth: Lawrence Kubie, with his timely encouragements; Gordon Allport, with his high expectations and unflinching *dis*couragements; and Elvin Semrad, who knew what I meant when I didn't—and said so.

*Waltham, Mass.*                                                    R.M.J.

# CONTENTS

*an application of*
## PSYCHOANALYSIS *to* EDUCATION

*CHAPTER ONE*

## SETTING - DESIGN - PROCEDURE

THE STUDY was carried out in a tradition bound New England preparatory boarding school for girls. Closely supervised regimentation of extracurricular activities permitted a minimum of individual differences in social interactions. The average I.Q. from year to year is about 110. The average age in the sample of the population studied was 17. The student population represents a very thin strata of society, all students coming from white upper middle and upper socio-economic families. The fathers of the majority of students are business executives. Although the students are drawn largely from the New England states all areas of the nation are represented. I shall refer to this school as the experimental school.

One of the control groups to be described was drawn from another girls' preparatory school in the same locality. It differs from the experimental school in being a somewhat more liberal day school catering largely to local professional families. In all other respects it is very similar to the experimental school. The atmosphere in both schools is one of keen awareness of social status. Competition for entrance into the "better" women's colleges is pressed. I shall refer to this school as the alternate school.

The homogenous nature of the research populations insured close inherent matching on age, sex, socio-economic position, intelligence, and educational level. In addition the commonly restricted life situation was conducive to close similarity of social experience during the experimental interval.

Both parts of the study relied upon the research design recommended by Allport (3) for evaluation research.

The paradigm was as follows:

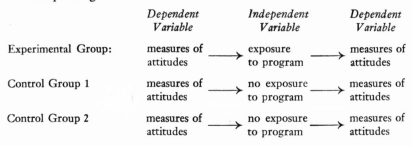

|  | Dependent Variable | Independent Variable | Dependent Variable |
|---|---|---|---|
| Experimental Group: | measures of attitudes | exposure to program | measures of attitudes |
| Control Group 1 | measures of attitudes | no exposure to program | measures of attitudes |
| Control Group 2 | measures of attitudes | no exposure to program | measures of attitudes |

The *experimental group* consisted of nineteen seniors in the experimental school who elected to be members of the Self-knowledge Workshops (to be described).

*Control Group* 1 consisted of nineteen seniors in the same school. The life experiences of these subjects during the experimental interval closely approximated the life experiences of the experimental subjects except that in place of the workshop the control subjects took an alternative elective course; either philosophy or Bible study. In addition these students were closely matched with the experimental subjects according to their initial scores on two of the dependent measures (to be described); namely, the E score and the NS score (see Table I). I shall refer to this group as the Matched Control Group.

TABLE I

INITIAL MEAN SCORES AND RANGES OF THE
MATCHED GROUPS ON MATCHING VARIABLES

| No. of Cases | Experimental Group 19 | Matched Control Group 19 |
|---|---|---|
| E Scale | | |
| Mean | 43.84 | 43.00 |
| Range | 52 | 57 |
| NS Score | | |
| Mean | 18.37 | 18.47 |
| Range | 26 | 25 |

*Control Group* 2 consisted of nineteen seniors randomly selected from the alternate school. The agreement with the alternate school did not permit the collecting of sufficient initial protocols to allow for matching on any of the dependent measures. This group was included in order to assess the possible indirect effects of the experimental program on the matched control subjects who, although not directly sharing the workshop experiences of the experimental subjects, could presumably have been *indirectly* influenced by way of informal communication. I shall refer to this group as the Alternate School Control Group.

## PROCEDURE

The following test battery was administered to the entire senior class of the experimental school and to a random third of the senior class of the alternate school at the beginning and at the end of one school year:

*Measures of Self-Acceptance*

1. *The Berger Scale for Self-Acceptance* (13) This is a paper and pencil self-rating type questionnaire in which the subject is asked to rate on a 1 to 5 scale from "true of myself" to "not at all true of myself" a series of statements that have been composed to reflect "self-acceptance."

   The resultant score (to be referred to as the Berger SA score) will be designated as a measure of conscious expressed attitudes of self-acceptance.

2. *The Dorris-Levinson-Hanfmann Sentence Completion Test* (27) The test was used in the form that is registered with the Photoduplication Service of the Library of Congress as Document No. 3979. Minor modifications were made in order to make the test applicable with female subjects.

   This is a first and third person paired-item sentence completion test presented to the subject as a "verbal speed test." In addition, the subject, after completing the test, is asked to indicate for each item whether the item as completed by him is true of himself or not.

   In an exploratory study (46) of this "Self-Reference Technique" the authors state:

   "Completions with negative (ego-threatening) content were denied self-reference significantly more frequently than were those with positive (ego-enhancing) content, which suggests that the "Non-self" judgment is often indicative of personal material that is either repressed or consciously denied."

This test is considered to combine certain features of the questionnaire technique and the projective technique and was therefore felt to be well suited to measure the changes in attitudes of self-acceptance that could realistically be expected to follow the workshop experience. It seems reasonable to assume that this test taps a deeper level of self-acceptance than does the Berger Scale. It yields the following measures:

*Non-self or NS score*—The number of responses that are denied self-reference.

*Ego-threatening or ET score*—The number of responses judged to be ego-threatening in nature.*

*Acceptance of ego-threatening responses or ET-A score*— The number of ego-threatening responses given self reference relative to the number of ego-threatening responses:

$$(\frac{ET\text{-}S}{ET} \times 100).$$

*Projectivity or NS-3 score*—The number of third person items denied self reference.

*Anti-intraception or NS-1 score*—The number of first person items denied self reference.

*Measures of Ethnic Attitudes*

3. *The Revised Bogardus Social Distance Scale* (11) The utility of this scale for measuring attitudes of ethnic prejudice is well known (11, 18, 19, 47, 74) and needs no documentation here.

4. *The Social Attitude Battery*—Included were the E, F, and TFI scales of the TAP Social Attitude Battery, Form FERPTI. Levinson (60) describes these scales as follows:

*The Ethnocentrism (E) Scale* deals with inter-group relations within this country and at the international level. High scores presumably indicate a generalized tendency to reject various out-groups such as Negroes, Jews, foreigners and other nations and to idealize the corresponding in-groups. Low scores are associated with rejection of both out-group prejudice and in-group idealization.

*The Authoritarianism (F) Scale* contains a variety of ideas concerning authority, work, sex, aggression, human nature and the like. High scores presumably indicate personality

* c.f. Appendix.

trends such as punitiveness, authoritarian, submission, stereo-
types, and projectivity.

*The Traditional Family Ideology (TFI) Scale* deals with
husband and wife relations, parent and child relations, conceptions of authority, masculinity and femininity and so on.
High scores indicate strong emphasis on discipline in child
training and on the dominant, assertive male and the rigidly
conventional female. Low scores indicate less dichotomous
definition of sex roles and greater emphasis on self expression.

The F and TFI Scales are not strictly speaking measures of
ethnic attitudes, but they have been demonstrated to be very
closely associated with the personality correlates of these attitudes.
They were included in the event of selective changes in this overall attitudinal syndrome.

It was hoped that such a variegated test battery would partially
compensate for the characteristic shortcomings of group testing,
both in terms of depth of attitudes being measured and in terms of
the breadth of the measuring methods.

The tests were administered in such a way as to keep them independent in the eyes of the subjects from the role of the workshop in the school setting. They were administered to the entire
senior class by persons who were not members of the faculty and
who were not known to the subjects. The tests were introduced
to the students by school authorities as a routine attempt to obtain
information necessary for the improvement of school services. The
students were assured that their responses would not be used in any
way that could personally affect them, and this assurance was
fortified by providing for anonymity in the taking of the tests.

The respective members of the experimental and control groups
were identified for purposes of pairing before and after protocols
by birth dates and other classificatory information. Once having
been properly categorized each case folder was assigned a code
number. Thereafter identification was exclusively by code number.

Following the second test administration the experimental subjects were asked to write an answer to the following questions: (1)
What effects do you feel your workshop experiences have had on
you? (2) To what extent do you feel that this course has dealt
with the topic of race prejudice? The purpose of the first question

was the collection of material for qualitative evaluation of the workshop. The purpose of the second question was to verify the "indirect" nature of the educational method in its relation to ethnic attitudes.

# PART ONE

## The Self-Knowledge Workshop

## CHAPTER TWO

# PERSPECTIVE

F ROM A POINT OF VIEW of strictest historical continuity the method to be described must be linked with the "Mental Hygiene" or "Human Relations" movements in American education. The advances made in these movements have not followed any single pattern. They seem rather to represent the more or less isolated efforts of diverse educators and psychologists who have brought to a commonly recognized need a wide range of theoretical orientations and technical innovations. Thus, without attempting to be exhaustive, we find that such workers as Slavson (90), Moreno (70), Strang (94), Bullis (21), Driver (29), and Seeley (86) have been active in the area. The methods used have included numerous variants of group discussion techniques, psychodrama techniques, counseling techniques, psychometric evaluation techniques, and home-grown didactic techniques. The titles covering such efforts range from "Human Relations Course" (including the "psychology" course that is secretly seeking to reap a psychotherapeutic harvest), through "Therapeutic Social Club," to the "How to Live" type of course.

Insofar as the Self-Knowledge Workshop is to be considered a member of this family of movements, I acknowledge the kinship by adding another "technique," and another catalog title (the title reluctantly until further refinements suggest something better). I also acknowledge the characteristic isolation of the contribution. This is to say that within the limitations of my awareness the method to be described was not influenced in its evolution by these other schools of experimentation.

On the other hand, the method **was** directly dependent; on the psychoanalytic movement in the assumptions that governed its planning; in the principles that guided its trials and errors; and in the theoretical framework within which it finds articulation. It is notable that Psychoanalysis, although more systematically coherent in itself than the efforts referred to above, has been less prominent than these efforts in its influence on American education.

The title "Self-Knowledge Workshop" reflects in part the influence of Lawrence Kubie who encouraged its development through personal communications and through his published writings. In a recent article (55) Kubie formulates a challenge which, he says, Psychoanalysis brings to the goals and techniques of education; namely, "education for wisdom," as well as for erudition. He states:

> As a result of the failure to consider the sources of error in the human being himself, when our academic disciplines assemble together . . . they reenforce the tacit, fallacious assumption that man can understand the world that lies outside of himself without concurrently understanding himself. Actually each man is his own microscope with his own idiosyncrasies, to which he alone can penetrate. Therefore we cannot perceive the outside world without distorting our very perceptions unless we search out individually the sources of error which lie hidden within. This is precisely what every mature discipline does in its own field; yet it is what no discipline does for the broad concept of education as a whole.

"Education for wisdom," states Kubie, " must close this gap by providing insight which penetrates into those areas of human life in which unconscious forces have always hitherto played the preponderant role." He acknowledges that to describe "self-knowledge in depth" as one of the goals of education is something quite other than its achievement. He offers no prescriptions beyond suggesting that meeting the challenge will require the development of basically new techniques of education, both for groups and for individuals, designed to integrate unconscious with conscious and preconscious processes.

The work of Elvin Semrad (87) and Leo Berman (15, 16) in adapting principles of psychoanalytic group psychotherapy to the teaching of professional training groups was directly influential in guiding the development of the Self-Knowledge Workshop. Dr. Semrad served as a consultant to the author in conducting the workshops during the experimental interval.

The author is the "instructor-leader" referred to in the descriptive accounts of the workshop that are to follow. At the beginning of the experimental interval, in addition to graduate academic training in clinical psychology, his relevant previous experience included having practiced group and individual psychotherapy, having been a member of a didactic training group, and having completed two years of personal psychoanalysis. During the preceding year the author had been employed by the experimental school as a psychology instructor. During this earlier year one class was offered a typical academic course, and in another an attempt was made to conduct group therapy as such. This was an unhappy experience which led to the conclusion that a method combining both the clinical group therapy approach and the traditional classroom approach was needed. Neither approach by itself seemed promising.

The group therapy approach seemed to collapse under the weight of the anxiety that is aroused and therefore under the weight of the unutilizable resistance. One could not approach normal persons in search of knowledge of themselves as though they were patients in search of relief from pain, Further, one could not interpret the consequent resistance as being displaced and expect a reduction of anxiety, as can be expected when the resistance does in fact reflect displacement. Anxiety was increased rather than decreased by such interpretations. This was taken as evidence that what was involved was not a displacement of resistance but a misplacement of method.

The traditional classroom approach, on the other hand, seemed inapplicable for the opposite reason. It became impoverished, for lack of anxiety, and therefore for lack of active resistance. Resistance, in an educational setting, seeming simply to be another term for ego involvement. Whatever was "learned" in such a setting was relegated inevitably to the emotional category of the "not me," and there was nothing in the agreed-on relationship between the student and the instructor that permitted the instructor to counter the process in the direction of a more personally involving kind of learning.

## CHAPTER THREE

# THEORY AND PLAN

THE ASSUMPTIONS that underlay the workshop **method** emanate
to a considerable extent from the speculative, untested edges of
systematic observation and theory building. Their exposition will
reflect the speculative nature of their source.

1. *Psychotherapy and education are overlapping but separately
definable processes.* Therapy, broadly defined, consists in restor-
ing the functioning of the ego to a state of "normality" that had
presumably been impaired by some form of compartmentalization in its organization of the symbolic processes. Education, ideally
defined, consists in insuring or allowing free play to the natural,
health-seeking symbolic processes of ego synthesis. From this point
of view, psychotherapy is a method for repairing damage resulting
from faulty or incomplete education. The specific techniques of
psychotherapy and of education are different—as, for example, are
the techniques of curing and remaining free from tuberculosis. The
differences, however, should not obscure our appreciation of the
common ground that supports both. This common ground takes
shape when we attempt to specify the above mentioned "natural,
health-seeking symbolic processes of ego synthesis."

From the observations of psychotherapists we note that greater
emotional freedom *and* control often follows the articulated entrance into consciousness of novel symbolic combinations—given
special interpersonal conditions that serve to focus attention on the
symbolic processes within an anxiety-reducing atmosphere. From
the observations of educators we note that what youngsters are al-
lowed in the presence of understanding authority to articulate to-

gether, in whatever symbolic forms, is never felt to be as dangerous, as guilt-inducing or as anxiety-provoking as the same experiences lived out in isolation. We note also that within such interactions the freedom of one individual to express what another individual inhibits often results in freeing the latter. This is known to extend to the capacity of children to make "depth interpretations"; i.e., to translate one another's expressive behavior into novel symbolic combinations that facilitate fresh insight.

We may add to this the observation of Allison Davis (26) that the anxieties and hostilities that are the natural consequences of the inevitable status relationships from birth on in all societies find their most fertile soil for reconciliation, as distinct from repression or uncontrolled expression, in the inter-relatings of age-mates.

2. *A group's interactions are potentially conducive to the psychological integration of its members.* This is not to say that all groups tend in this direction, nor is it to imply that we know enough about group dynamics to specify with precision what conditions of group interaction create and nurture this potential. My own experience suggests that it is most effectively brought into play by a working pedagogical rule of thumb that a group of individuals is very closely analogous to a single individual as regards its having a distinct personality with a beginning and an end, internal needs, external expectations within whose confines the needs are to be met, and certain mechanisms for integrating (or compartmentalizing) the symbolic representations of these life ingredients during its life span. Moreover, it is assumed that if such a group entity becomes more integrated during its life span it is a reflection of changes in the individual personalities who, through mutual identification, have *been* "the group personality." A group that becomes more itself does so only by way of its members becoming more *themselves*, and yet the processes to be observed are not those that we are accustomed to see operating in either psychotherapy or education, considered alone. One group of adolescents, for example, reacted to what it initially considered the leader's "un-teacherlike approach" by becoming greatly concerned with its autonomy as a group. It consolidated its autonomous position in relation to the leader by introducing ("for the sake of a little dignity instead of all

these emotions") a seminar table into its meetings, which was thereafter referred to as "our barricade." For months afterward the "barricade" served as an omnipresent symbolic representation of the members' ambivalences in regard to feelings of security vs. feelings of intimacy in their relations with one another and with grown-ups—and in relation to their own individually defensive ways of resolving these ambivalences. And on the day when this group decided to do without the seminar table (as a "superfluous prop") the leader was privileged to witness a discussion of the free will vs. determinism controversy that was more intimately searching and intellectually rich than will be found in the colloquia of many graduate schools.

Another group reacted to the same situation by spontaneously, in one of the middle meetings, dispensing with the chairs and sitting in a closed circle at the leader's feet, with accompanying associations to grandfathers and story-telling, and feelings of "coyness." Later, after ventilating hostile feelings toward a leader who would not sit on the floor with them, this group reflected that the move was "a groupy way of breaking through the don't care front." For a while it "left us feeling like children, but it was one way of admitting we were all in the same boat and cared."

A corollary consideration pertains to the functional role of the person who undertakes to be the "understanding authority" in the group. If the leader of such a group has been psychoanalytically trained he finds the temptation strong to exploit the quantitative nature of the situation to the end of maintaining a series of simultaneous therapeutic relationships. While this may well be a usefully economic approach to some clinical goals, it would seem to represent questionable economy if carried over to the pursuit of educational goals. If, as Davis' work testifies, the peer group has a natural and qualitatively different potential for stimulating and supporting mutual ego synthesis in its members, then the leader would best serve as the originator and protector of the group's integrity—and therefore as the object for the focusing of parent-transference—rather than as the well-meaning usurper of its potential.

3. *"Reality" is educational.* In this context we refer to the *external*, observable "reality" of interpersonal relations. In a sense this

assumption is a counterpoint to that which posits "natural, health-seeking forces of ego synthesis," i.e., the internal, unobservable "reality" of *intra*personal relations. This is a notion that has more of a place in psychoanalytic therapy than in psychoanalytic theory. Kubie makes this assumption articulate as follows (57):

> The symbols by which we think are multivalent tools, al ways representing many things simultaneously, some conscious, some preconscious, and some unconscious. In logical thinking, the conscious and pre-conscious symbolic processes represent external reality without disguises. What we call "logic" there-fore is in essence a coding of relationships which are inherent among such internal and external data as are accessible to our direct perceptual processes. One might almost say that although logic resides in the mind, its roots are in the relations among external facts themselves. It is a neglected consequence of this principle, that it is literally impossible to be "illogical" about ac-cessible data except when one has an unconscious axe to grind.

All this is not to say that reality *misperceived* is educational. It *is* to say that to confront a student's misperceptions of social reality with the external facts of that reality, and to expect that corrected perceptions will eventually follow, is as sound pedagogy as telling a mathematics student that his answer to a problem is incorrect, and expecting his review of the facts to have a naturally corrective in-fluence. The math student, however, has his books, and his notes, which he accepts as representing the clearly perceivable realities of mathematics, and which do indeed represent these realities so far as they have been clearly perceived. The question is: If we aim to "teach" self-knowledge, are there comparable points of reality reference?

4. *The representations of social realities are the agreements that people make with one another.* The agreement may be clearly or vaguely perceived. It may represent the actual realities of people's wishes, and of their capacities to realize their wishes, or it may rep-resent distortions of these realities. Agreements are what people enter into with their egos, i.e., with that system of personality that is equipped to consciously accept or reject, to perceive or distort, and to correct distortion—i.e., to *learn*. It is a reality-based agree-ment that enables a therapist constructively to interpret his patient's

distortions, and to refer him to his life experiences for correction. It it a reality-based agreement that enables a mathematics teacher to point out his student's error, and to refer him to the book. It would seem therefore that it will also be a reality-based agreement of some kind that will support the "teaching" of self-knowledge. Consequently, to undertake such "teaching" is to accept the responsibility of presenting an agreement that does indeed represent the realities of "learning" self-knowledge. The math teacher who refers his student to a fallacious book is a misleading teacher. If he is aware that the book is fallacious he must either procure a more realistic book or write a better one. He must, in other words, vouch with his own integrity for the accuracy of what he offers as representing reality. The "teacher" of self-knowledge is doubly handicapped in these respects. On the one hand, at the present stage of our development in this area, he is behooved to "write the book," if he is to have any assurance of being himself able to read it. On the other hand, the probability is inevitably high that he himself will not be aware of the distortions he has written into it. We must not, therefore, underestimate the challenge involved in using agreements in this way. Agreements between people are notoriously fraught with short-sightedness and mal-perception of the facts of human nature.

If an agreement that undertakes the deepening of self-awareness is to be presented to students, and upheld as representing the realities involved in such an enterprise, it cannot be a casually constructed agreement. To carry out such an educational enterprise one is called upon, in the spirit of one of the traditionally unverbalized components of the "analytic attitude," to wear the mantle of absolutism comfortably and in good conscience. This being the case it would seem that one's preparation for such an undertaking would include at least a thorough study of human nature, including that study of one's *own* human nature that insures, as much as is possible, that one's own view of human realities will be free at least from habitual and repetitive personal distortions.

5. *The neurotic process in ubiquitous.* I am not assuming by this that *neurosis* (the spiraling, repetitive way of life) is universal. I am assuming that there is in the development of the ego a natural ten-

dency toward compartmentalization of symbolic processes which, once stabilized, will meet a catalytic influence with resistance. This need not mushroom into the malignancy that the analyst treats. The natural underlying condition that supports this tendency would seem to be the structural incongruities that are inherent in the development of human thought organization; i.e., in the vicissitudes of inter-communication between what we have come to specify as the primary and secondary systems of thought organization; between, in Langerian terms (59), the sphere of "presentational" symbols and the sphere of "discursive" symbols; in more immediately relevant terms between the idiom of dreams and idiom of "study habits." These systems, we know, are essentially *inter*dependent, and sanctioned as such in the "integrated" personality, but we also know they are of such mutually incongruous quality as to readily support the illusion of *in*dependence. Taking advantage of this readiness for illusion is perhaps the most universally accepted of fallacious agreements; namely, that since the experiences deriving from the primary process are not rational, and are not manipulable by the more familiar mechanisms of conscious regulation, they are not real.

How often, for example, do we hear the young child who has not yet been "educated" into this illusion, told that what he presents as a richly meaningful experience was "*only* a dream!" How then can he be expected to adapt to this experience of self by any process but some form of compartmentalization (for example; therefore it is not me; or, it is me, but it is *only* me). This kind of "education" is, as we know, extended and greatly reinforced by existing educational practices, where "disciplining the mind" seeks almost invariably to exclude from the ego's sanctioning influence the non-discursive symbol, the irregular experience, the novel connection—this in its one-sided dedication to the discursive symbol, the conforming experience, the obligatory connection. From this point of view it is impossible to avoid the sobering conclusion that formal education, as we know it, is in its fundamental assumptions, neurotogenic. In other words, while the "knowledge" carried in the more focused forms of the secondary process is, in reality, an economical refinement of the more concrete and more fluid "knowledge" of the primary process, the capacity for ego-synthesis in respect to these interdependent qualities of knowledge is almost universally undermined in the name of education. To attempt the reverse the neurotic process, we know, is to encounter resistance. As testimony to this is the author's experience, in the process of attempting to apply these principles in the classroom, of witnessing groups of so-called rebellious adolescents demanding in urgent tones to be "taught," to be required to make sense, to be given more tests and more assignments!

6. The sixth assumption follows Schactel (84) in his classical refinement of the psychoanalytic theory of repression. This position states: *repression is not exclusively the traumatic consequence of tabooed content experiences, but is also a consequence of generally impoverished mode experiences.* In discussing the phenomenon of infantile amnesia Schactel adds to Freud's concept of the repression of specifically objectionable infantile material, the concept of culturally induced repression of the infantile mode of experiencing. These two types of repression he views at two ends of a continuum. Childhood experiences are "trans-schematic" experiences, rich in the quality of fresh sensual discovery. Adult experiences are schematic experiences limited by the capacity of culturally approved linguistic, conceptual, and memory schemata to contain them. Schactel's key concept is the memory mechanism of "conventionalization": recalling the schemata of experiences rather than recalling the experiences themselves. These schemata being culturally preformed, any experience that transcends them is in danger of being lost because there exists no "vessel" to contain it. Herein lies, for Schactel, the efficacy of psychoanalytic free association: it encourages "non-schematic" experiences.

Schactel's thinking closely parallels the more familiar psychoanalytic theorizing with respect to the primary and secondary systems of thought organization, and is in accord with our assumption in respect to the ubiquity of the neurotic process. His bi-modal understanding of repression, however, is unique, and there is very little evidence bearing on it at present. My own speculations run as follows: if repression is referable to a continuum denoted at one end by the loss of knowledge due to specifically anxiety-provoking associations, and at the other by the loss of knowledge due to the unavailability of appropriate vehicles for its containment, then it is reasonable to assume that the two types of repression are mutually facilitative; that repression of certain tabooed material, for example, would not be necessary to an individual's psychic economy if the symbolizing tools necessary for its reorganization were not also in a different sense taboo. If the first type of repression is reversible, or at least reorganizable, as we know it is, albeit not readily, then it is conceivable that the second type (i.e., conventionalization) may also be reversible. The strategic question is whether or not the latter may be *more readily* reversible within educational settings. To regress to meta-psychology for a moment, we may speculate that the supergo would take a more benign attitude toward lifting of the *conventionally* repressed than toward lifting of the *specifically* repressed, and this in turn would provide the ego with the tools to soften the superego's harshness with regard to certain features of the *specifically* repressed. Such speculation, of course, raises a host of theoretical issues which it is not our purpose to resolve in the present context. Suffice to say that the author has found many students surprisingly ready—even eager—to overcome their own initial resistance to the meaningfulness of the *forms* in which their unconscious experiences can take shape, and that this readiness did not extend to the contentual aspects of these experiences.

7. *Not only do personality structures formed in one's past influence the experiencing of one's present, but the experiencing of one's present may re-form the personality structures formed in one's past.* This is an assumption that derives from recent extensions of psychoanalytic ego psychology associated with the works of Hartmann (77), Kris (54), Rapaport (77), and Erikson (30)—especially from Hartmann's thinking as regards "neutralization" and the interaction between the "conflict" and "conflict-free" ego spheres.

Such an assumption has, of course, always been inherent in the psychoanalytic understanding of the phenomena of "transference" and "working through of the transference." Analysts have always viewed the "transference neurosis" as the pivotal experience around which a really re-educative process may take place. Hartmann's terminology simply enables us to consider the process more systematically. What has not been sufficiently thought through, I think, is the fact that transference, the very phenomenon that makes the analytic re-living and re-learning an emotional reality, is itself an experience in the present. The question germane to our immediate interest is whether the re-integrative potential inherent in transference processes can be as imaginatively harnessed to teacher-student and student-student relationships as they were by their discoverer to the doctor-patient relationship.

As long as this question was not raised psychoanalysis and education were insular to one another. Vital personality change was reserved to analysands. Allport's concept of "functional autonomy" (4) seems in retrospect to have endeared itself to our intuitive understanding of human nature precisely because it drew off some of the tension that generated from around the periphery of this blind spot—but it did so by denying the fundamental premise (that personality development is historically continuous) on which the conceptual model of psychoanalytic theory is based, instead of refining the premise.

Rapaport (77) has rescued both the premise and Allport, with his refined concept of *"relative* functional autonomy." What I mean to underscore in the present context is that the very extensions of the theory which lead Rapaport to the conclusion that the *functions* of the ego may become relatively autonomous of their previous alliances with id, superego, and immaturely perceived reality, simultaneously require the conclusion that the *dysfunctions* of the ego are, in a similar sense, relative in their autonomy—in this connection in their autonomy in respect to the influences of an enlightened conscience and of maturely perceived reality. Relative, I here venture to add, to the opportunities for re-integration that a person's environment affords him through exercise of those preconscious symbolic representations of the ego-dystonic unconscious, which are themselves, however circuitously, ego-syntonic.

The assumptions that underlay the approach to the workshop MEMBERS emanate from the more substantiated body of orthodox psychoanalytic theory.

The girls' normal development was viewed along psychosexual and psychosocial dimensions. "Normal" development was defined as that state of ego organization in which the structural adaptation (sexual identity, choice of defenses, etc.) is in accord with the realistic possibilities for libidinal adaptation—in other words when the fantasies which the ego accepts as a challenge to its synthesis and reality testing functions are ultimately capable of fulfillment in reality.

Along the psychosexual dimension Freud (40, 41, 42) led the way with his outline of libidinal development, which states that it corresponds to the successive maturation of the oral-sensory, anal-muscular, and genital-locomotor apparatuses. This is to say that the child's significant interpersonal relations, his fantasies about them, and his attempts to comprehend and to master them, are intimately linked during these early times with his significant *intra*-personal relations with his own person (his "body" ego), his fantasies about *it*, and his attempts to comprehend and to master *it*. Thus the Freudian shorthand in which "oral," "anal," "phallic," "vaginal," etc., denote *models* which in turn connote intricate *modes* of activity, i.e., structured possibilities for libidinal discharge.

Along the psychosocial dimension Erikson (30, 31) led the way with his basic outline of ego development, which states that insofar as the child's inter- and intra-personal relations are not excessive or unrealistic in respect to the demands they make of one another—insofar, that is, as he is permitted to integrate his social and biological heritage—the child successfully resolves to that extent a series of basic life issues. In the pre-oedipal period there arise the issues of "basic trust vs. basic mistrust," and "autonomy vs. shame and doubt;" in the oedipal period, "initiative vs. guilt;" in the latency period, "industry vs. inferiority;" and in adolescence "ego identity vs. ego diffusion." This is too paltry a coverage of Erikson, in whose hands psychoanalytic theory takes shape, I believe, as the key to eventual success in deepening education. As we have yet to comprehend the lock, however, I must put off the development of this belief to another time.

As regards the broad outline of ego development, no distinction is made between the sexes. The artful and individually stylized forms which we know individual resolutions of these issues to take are, of course, infinite—if anything is infinite. The abstract nature of the issues themselves, however, and the human ego "apparatus" for resolving them, we assume to be the same for both sexes. Where the sexes differ, is in the respective demands placed upon them by "normality," previously defined as that state of organization in which the structural adaptation is in accord with the realistic possibilities for libidinal development, i.e., with the libidinal models that do in fact exist.

Thus the immense significance in a child's development of the oedipus and castration complexes. For it is at this point that the child, almost necessarily always alone with his thoughts, must decisively come to grips with the sobering fact of differences in human affairs—differences in size, differences in strength, differences in talents and in the opportunities for their expression, mystifying differences from moment to moment in his own pattern of emotional loyalties and disloyalties—all as most compellingly brought home to him by the tantalizing fact of differences in sex. Here the ego must take stock, as it were, of the fantasies it has thus far entertained, and *choose* which it will accept as the real challenge of the future, and which it will relegate to the nostalgia of things once rawly desired, but never to be possessed in the raw. We know that the child mightily resists this choice under the natural pressure of wishing to choose both, and that the nub of his resistance is his refusal to see it as a choice at all (the castration complex), and that he only reluctantly ventures to make a choice when he sees hope attached to being more like one parent than the other (the oedipus complex). Thus normality hangs in the balance of the oedipal crotch, so to say, when the child's biological model for possibilities of libidinal discharge pits the strength of its yet amorphously dimensioned impulses with or against the private view of the future represented by his two parents.

Briefly, then, during the pre-oedipal period of **libidinal** development from the beginning of her sexual life to around three years of age the girl's major fantasies closely parallel the boy's. The primary love object is the mother toward whom there are conflicting passive and active libidinal strivings. The father is viewed as the rival for the mother's affection, for the girl as well as for the boy, and the basic wish-theme (disregarding variations) is the same: to give mother a baby. Thus both boy and girl play out their destiny-oriented struggles with the issues of basic trust and personal autonomy around these fantasies as influenced by similar oral and anal impulses.

With the end of the pre-oedipal period, at the maturational awakening of the phallic genital, which ushers in the intense phase of infantile sexuality, the demands of normal development differ as the natural possibilities of the respective phallic genitals differ. Here the girl is expected to develop a feeling of personal initiative without benefit of the boy's readily visible biological model of initiative. Her childish fantasies tell her that she may still by some aggressive or seductive means acquire a penis, which at this stage becomes vaguely equated with the previous wish for a baby. At the oedipal crisis, as the boy, under threat of castration by the father, renounces his phallic claim to the mother in favor of a more promising future, the girl views her mother's "castration" as the final blow to her hopes of acquiring a penis, turns from the source of previous supply toward the father as a new love object, transfers her wish for a penis-baby to him, and the mother now becomes the rival. The normal girl tends to remain in this phase of the oedipus complex *until* (and this is the crucial point that psychoanalytic female psychology has tended to overlook) *slowly* she comes to discover her own model for adequate feminine initiative (the vagina), at which she retains the realistic wish for a baby, and renounces the unrealistic and now superfluous wish for a penis. Thus, having met the demands of normality by renouncing the impossible and choosing the possible, she insures her freedom to continue exercising active choice in her post-oedipal stages of development.

We know that the castration and oedipus complexes are not once solved and never again re-solved. Rather, the essence of the successful oedipal resolution is the capacity to re-solve it at every subsequent stage of emotional development, wherever ambivalence is encountered. Much later, when the issues of industry and ego-identity have been met, in turn successfully resolved, and integrated with the oedipal resolution, we say that the individual is "genital" in character.

Thus we expect to find the members of the workshop who are presumably intensely involved in the adolescent contest between ego identity and ego diffusion preconsciously re-reviewing that which in fantasy may have been unrealistically renounced, and that which may have been unrealistically preserved.

Theory, when translated into a blueprint for action, emerged as follows:

1. The students are to be confronted with a model choice situation in the form of an agreement that represents as accurately as is possible the "realities" of mature social intercourse, and of the processes of gaining the prerequisite depth of self-awareness. The agreement is to be offered as a contract which the student is free to accept or to reject, thus enlisting the cooperation of the learning ego. Once having accepted the terms of the agreement, however, thus earning its *privileges*, the student is constantly to be expected by the workshop authority to meet its *responsibilities*, thus insuring the introduction into the processes of student-instructor interaction the phenomena of resistance and transference.

2. The terms of the agreement and its implementation by the workshop authority should encourage the verbal articulation of the resistance and the transference—and therefore of previously unintegrated parts of the self.

3. The traumatic effect on late adolescents of being tacitly assumed capable of genital adequacy, although not unrealistic, is calculated to insure regression in the reaction of the students, thus creating the possibility of constructively influencing in a very real sense an emotional recapitulation of previous emotional development.

4. To the end of bringing a constructive influence to bear on this recapitulatory experience the following rules of technique were formulated in advance:

(1) Outlets for "safe" acting out of the regression should be provided for by the inclusion of traditional educational aims and practices.

(2) The "group" should be considered the instrument of therapeutic influence. The group leader's objective as the transference figure should be to uphold the agreement, to encourage the focusing of consequent expressions of hostility upon the transference figure, and to encourage, support, and protect the integrity of the group.

(3) Specifically repressed unconscious content should not be dealt with. The emphasis should rather be on uncovering and integrating the preconscious representations of this content and upon the meaningfulness of the *idiom* of non-conscious symbolic processes, i.e., the conventionally repressed.

## CHAPTER FOUR

## NARRATIVE

THE COURSE was entered in the school bulletin as follows:

SELF-KNOWLEDGE WORKSHOP — The aim of this course is increased self-understanding for the girl herself. The principal work consists of supervised intensive small-group discussion. Mastery of psychological subject matter is encouraged only insofar as it aids the processes of mastering personal life-history subject matter. Enrollment is limited to twenty students in two sections of ten each. Senior elective. Four appointments weekly.

At the first session, copies of "The Agreement" were distributed to each student, read, and discussed. It read as follows:

## SELF-KNOWLEDGE WORKSHOP
## FULL CREDIT COURSE; FOUR CLASS PERIODS PER WEEK

This is an *elective* course, which means that you are free to choose or to decline membership in it. In order to make your decision wisely, you will want to know more about it:

The aim of the Workshop will be to increase and to deepen your understanding of yourself. Experience tells us that no one has ever deepened his self-knowledge without experiencing, somewhere along the line, a certain amount of anxiety and personal discomfort. To point out also that no one who has ever truly deepened his understanding of self has regretted these discomforts is in no way to deny that they are real ones.

How often have we heard or used the expression: "If only I could just be myself?" Now, it would seem, on the surface of it, that "being one's self" should be the easiest thing in life to be.

In fact, however, it is the most difficult task a person can undertake. Most of us are engaged in it in some vague way a good deal of the time anyhow, but it is doubly difficult all by ourselves. Perhaps you have noticed in your own life that there are times when you find yourself acting in ways that you, yourself, do not like; or *not* acting in ways that you *do* like. Perhaps you have noticed these things in the form of minor day to day conflicts that seem to get repeated, or perhaps in the form of major life crises that had you baffled for a time. The point is not that we all have such things in our lives. We *must* have them, in order to grow as persons. The point is that in some instances we do not know how to learn from them; and by this learning, do something about them; and by this doing, grow more closely toward what we really, deep-down, want to become.

It will be the task of the Workshop, therefore, not to rid you of your conflicts nor to help you to make light of your times of crisis, but rather to help you to find in yourself, and then to perfect, the natural tools that enable people confidently to deal with these things, and to put *all* of their life experiences (happy and unhappy) into the service of becoming their real selves.

So you see, your choice is not an idle one, because our purpose in working together will have a note of personal earnestness about it that may not have been present in the school courses you have had in the past—which, however, is not to say that we may not have our moments of fun together. If you choose to become a member of the Workshop, plan to bring to it more than just your "school self." If you choose not to become a member, there can be no blame in not taking an elective course.

The following is a rough outline of what you may expect to find in the workshop:*

1. Class time will be divided into two forty-minute periods and one eighty-minute period per week.

2. Most forty-minute periods will be devoted to topical group discussion, the topics to be based on assigned or suggested reading materials or on personal experiences of common interest.

* Not included in the pre-formulated agreement, although, as it turned out, crucial to its maintenance, was the instructor's plan that the subject-focused class meetings be held around a seminar table, and the free-discussion group meetings in an open circle of chairs. The importance of the arrangement becomes clear later.

3. Some forty-minute periods will be devoted to lectures on technical subjects by the instructor.

4. All eighty-minute periods will be devoted to free-discussion group meetings. These will be conducted so as to give each workshop member an opportunity to know herself in relation to the other group members in an atmosphere of freedom especially designed for this purpose.

Experience has shown that the members may expect to gain more from the free-discussion meetings, the more they refrain from carrying the discussions over into non-group situations. This will prove to be an even greater handicap if indulged with non-group members. Boarding school life being what it is, this will prove to be a difficult rule to observe. It is nevertheless strongly recommended.

The instructor agrees to keep the content of all group meetings, and of all ungraded written work, in strict professional confidence. This will apply in all of his dealings—professional and otherwise—with school administrators, teachers, students, and parents.

You may feel free, therefore, in these meetings, to express yourself on any matter that is a source of concern, or just plain interest to you. In short, as long as you can put it in words, anything goes.

## Workshop Requirements

1. To observe regulations that apply to regular school courses.
2. To complete all assignments.
3. To see to it, as a group, that a written set of minutes of each free-discussion meeting is presented to the group at the beginning of each succeeding free-discussion meeting.

The point was emphasized in this first session that it was entirely possible and understandable if some students had signed up for the course expecting a course in psychology or something else quite different from what they were now being led to expect. At the end of the session the instructor stated that he did not consider attendance at the first session to in any way signify formal academic commitment, and that the school administration also took this position. The students were encouraged, therefore, to reconsider their motives in view of what they were being asked to agree to, and to continue their enrollment only if they wanted to make such an agreement. They could indicate their acceptance of it by attending the next session.

All who were present at the first sessions chose to accept the terms of the agreement and thus to make their enrollment academically binding. It was clear that for most of the members the agreement was viewed as one of the unpredictable quirks that must be expected of teachers; and that the act of exercising autonomous choice in the matter was of the "theirs not to reason why" variety —despite the reality of actually having made a choice. On the contrary it was soon very clear that at the very time the choice itself was being made the emotional stages were being set for the expected familiar struggle between students and teacher—in which students (finding that the struggle is real by virtue of never having had a choice) are encouraged to isolate their choice-making ego behind the familiar facades of superficial conformity **and** therefore superficial rebellion.

In documenting what followed I have attempted to highlight the perceptual distortions of the agreement, the forms of group resistance and group transference, the topics discussed, the fantasies expressed, and the preconscious emotional recapitulation that could be inferred from these. The nature of these processes seemed best communicated by a running narrative of the development of one of the workshops in its free-discussion meetings. The parts played in this development by the shorter class meetings will be taken up later. In formulating this account I have drawn freely upon my own retrospective notes, the members' minutes, and verbatim tape recordings of each meeting in that sequence which seemed to serve communication best.*

The flavor of the first meeting from the viewpoint of the group itself is conveyed by the minutes of this meeting:

### FREE DISCUSSION—NO. 1

At the beginning of the period the floor was open for suggestions as to what we wanted to discuss in our first free discussion

---

* G stands for a member of the group. What follows is verbatim. L stands for group leader. What follows is verbatim.
Bracketed statements are condensations of the author's observations.

period. Mr. J. was asked what he wanted. He referred us to the agreement. The discussion was begun by the suggestion that we talk about dreams and that dreams could be divided into classes of fear and desire. Po. asked if Mr. J. would psychoanalyze us and tell us about ourselves at the end of the year. Ga. answered for him by saying that he was going to help us do it ourselves.

The class as a whole was very confused as to what our assignments were to be for the discussion. We decided on an alphabetical system for taking minutes. The questions that were asked were: Were we each to write a summary after every discussion period or a report and would we fail the course if we didn't, as it was evident that Mr. J. was not going to tell us the assignment? Were we to take notes in class? All Mr. J. said was that we seemed not to have remembered our agreement. Someone suggested that we take notes on what was a help to us.

Mr. J. brought up the fact that the memory was a tricky thing and asked if we thought there was a reason for gaps in our memories. These questions helped to change the mood of the class but no decision was made about assignments. Several of us complained that we weren't getting anywhere.

Next we took up the subject of dreams. Someone told of dreams in which you did later what you dreamt and didn't remember the dream until you had started the task. Also the theory of reincarnation was brought into the dreams. Someone explained to the class that if you were in a place where you had never been before and yet you knew where to go, you would have known it from a past life. In other words, you were reincarnated. Someone asked if you believed in spiritualism would you still believe in God? Je. brought up the fact that people who believed in Buddhism centuries ago believed in one God and still believed in reincarnation. These people believed that they were reincarnated in order to become better people and eventually find peace and become one with Nirvana. Nirvana was the name they gave to the one God that they believed in. Po. said that she knew of a woman who had three husbands and couldn't be happy with any of them. She believed that she had been a bad person in her past life and she was paying for it now. La. asked if it were true that you never hit bottom in a dream and did this mean that you were unsure of yourself? Others asked if people who dreamed in color were insane? Do you dream about the things you do just before you go to sleep? Was it true that Freud believed that every dream is related in some way to sex? Mr. J. said that these questions would be dealt with later on in the course. He also said that dream interpretation was both a very tricky and a very simple business, that the best interpreter of a dream was the dreamer, but that outside hints could be helpful. He emphasized that although dreams were in a funny language they were very real, very important and always meaningful.

People said that they had had dreams that seemed so vivid that they believed that they were true, or about hearing noises or being bitten by a dog, or seeing people materialize. Ba. told of a dream in which her sister screamed and it coincided with her own dream. Li. asked if it were possible for best friends to dream the same thing at the same time. Po. said that dreams are dangerous. Ba. said that she has only horrible dreams. Mr. J. asked what was the most frightening thing about dreams. We thought it was the awareness of what could happen. We asked if he would interpret our dreams and tell us about them. He said that we would probably find that his interpretations would only clutter up our own thinking about our dreams.

Mr. J. went back to the theory of reincarnation and asked us where we had gotten the theory. We said that we assumed it to be true. Mr. J. said that assumptions were good things to have because they were what self-confidence came from but that they were only good if they could face the facts. The facts here were that we had agreed on our aims and the means for reaching them, but that we now seemed very unsure of where we were going and of how to get there. He said that when people were unsure of themselves they tried to feel more sure in short cut ways that prevented them from discovering what they were really unsure about—ways like making quick assumptions or setting up a boss to tell them what to be sure of. He thought that when we got to know each other beter we would find other ways of feeling sure. The bell rang.

Thus in the first meeting the group attempted to initiate a childhood relationship with an unknown authority. When the authority did not cooperate the reaction of the group was to conform nontheless to what little it knew of his interests. When this too failed we note signs of uneasiness, of regression to infantile modes of absolutistic and moralistic thought. We also note associations that smack of rebirth fantasies. It is as if in the very process of encountering new fears new hopes are raised. The leader responds by focusing on the preconscious feelings of uncertainty and inadequacy, thus objectifying the fear, and supporting the group in its capacity to hope.

The *second* meeting opens with self-punitive expressions of boredom and irritation with the previous meeting.

**G:** We didn't get anywhere.

**L:** Why?

**G:** You wouldn't tell us the assignments.

**L:** Are we all in agreement now?

**G:** Let's not go back to that again!

**L:** Why?

**G:** It isn't what you do in a class.

**G:** You (leader) may gain something but we don't.

**L:** Do you mean you made an agreement that left you out in the cold?

**G:** He can tell us later in the year.

**G:** No, tell us *now*.

**G:** It was our fault that we didn't get anywhere.

**L:** What *was* the problem last time?

**G:** Oh, no, not again!

(The group rehashes the last meeting looking for the source of irritation. It decides that it was the fact that no conclusions were reached.)

**G:** Did you say we can say anything we want?

**L:** As long as you can put it in words, anything goes. (You can express anything you can control.)

**G:** Who has a problem? (Jokingly)

**G:** What about a person who panics when she loses anything. I have a friend . . .

**G:** (according to the minutes):

Je. brought up the subject of a girl she knows who gets panicky whenever she loses anything. She asked if anyone could think of a reason for this panic. Po. thought maybe the girl had few possessions and valued each one highly. Li. suggested that maybe her parents were very strict about her losing things. No one came up with any reason that was particularly well supported by the class. Mr. J. came up with a question asking what did the group feel was missing in these meetings. Po. questioned Mr. J.'s reason for asking such questions. Mr. J. said that he was using the freedom of the group to say whatever he wanted to.

**G:** I thought of losing things in connection with forgetting our assignment.

**L:** What is it we're not sure of here that we always have been sure of?

**G:** Ourselves!

**G:** A teacher!

**G:** It's odd to have a teacher that just sits there. A teacher is usually entirely present or entirely absent.

**G:** What *do* you (leader) want?

**G:** Will you tell us why people forget things?

**L:** Yes, in the next *class* meeting.

**G:** Why not now?

**L:** That is not what we agreed to do together in the group meetings.

**G:** But you're the one who knows everything.

**G:** He doesn't know *every*thing.

**G:** What *are* we supposed to discuss in this period?

**L:** When it comes to self-knowledge the word "suppose" is probably the most famous last word of all famous last words.

(The group launches into a lively and disorganized period of trying to decide what "he meant by that.")

**G:** In other words we don't think *our* answers are worth anything.

**G:** What we're supposed to do here is to find out our problems and discuss them.

**G:** Nobody ever sounds sure of what they say here.

**G:** I've got an idea. Maybe it's because in other classes we're used to having an authority. Here there are no particular authorities but ourselves. (A good intellectual insight, but easier said than felt.)

(The group takes up a long discussion of liquor and its effect on the mind and why people drink. There are references to "emotions," "opening up," "letting down barriers," "longing to be loved," "nightmares," "the guilty morning after," etc.)

**L:** Some people drink too much simply because they haven't yet learned how to know people well without it.

**G:** Will you help us? Tell us what liquor does to a person!

**L:** How alcohol chemically affects the brain is something we can take up in class. (An explosive group expression of affectionately toned exasperation with the leader)

**G:** We don't accomplish anything this way.

**L:** I think you're accomplishing a great deal.

**G:** You do? What?

**L:** Do you really and truly want to understand yourselves? It takes a while.

**G:** What we've been doing brings other people's opinions out into the open.

**L:** Why is that an accomplishment?

**G:** It means you can bring some of *yours* out too.

**G:** Maybe when we talk about other people we really mean ourselves.

**L:** This can be risky before we know each other quite well.

**G:** Yes!

(The group continues with the liquor discussion and concludes that one can't be himself under the influence of liquor. The topic then shifts to habitual drinkers with obvious personal family relevance on the part of one girl. She baits the group until she is asked who she is referring to, at which she asks the leader if he wants her to say who it is. The leader hears this as an attempt at seducing him into accepting the group's insecurely carried responsibility for discovering the implications of the agreement.)

**L:** Do you *want* to tell us?

**G:** Don't tell us unless you *want* to!

(She doesn't, and the topic continues around "this man" and why he may drink so much: "searching for something," "something missing within himself," "feels insecure."

**L:** If we follow our agreement, will this make us drunk?

**G:** We're not going to lower ourselves—not just be unkind to people.

**L:** (to the taker of the minutes) Will you be able to read between the lines and tell us something about ourselves from this meeting?

**G:** For a group of people who know each other as little as we do we certainly went places today. We haven't come out and said *everything* but we've said more than we would if we were just having a bull session by ourselves.

**G:** Yes, but we made an agreement that these meetings would be confidential. We *have to trust* each other.

**L:** That is mainly an assumption so far, isn't it?

**G:** We've seen that no one got hurt and there was an opportunity to hurt us and no one did.

**G:** I think we're opening up more.

**L:** I think you're wise in going slow. It takes a while to test these things out.

**G:** We test out the same way at home—not just here.

**G:** There are many ways of finding out if you can trust people.

**L:** Yes, and I daresay we'll be using many ways we never knew we had before.

**G:** (Laughingly) Do *you* (leader) trust us?

As the members were leaving, the tape recorder picked up this interchange: "These meetings certainly show we're interested in other people." "In other people or in ourselves?" . . . "He'd be surprised!" . . . "These meetings could have an effect on our lives!"

At this early stage in the group's development the associational content is marked by "oral" references. The transference is still that of the dependent child seeking anaclitic harmony with the supposedly omnipotent adult, but is now being questioned. The corresponding resistances center around the directing of hostility inward. As the hostility begins to find a less costly object in the leader we note that it is propped upon the erroneous justification that "this is not what you do in a class."

With the group's defenses well established and the feeling of group identity taking root the way is paved for insightfully resolving the first major developmental issue, i.e., basic trust versus basic mistrust—the very language with which the group itself spontaneously clothes the issue. We do not, of course, expect this issue to be resolved in a few meetings, nor to be completely resolved in any number of meetings, nor to be worked through in more articulate ways without occasional strategic regressions to less articulate ways. We *do* expect that it will be resolved sufficiently to free the energy needed to re-face and to re-integrate to individually varying degrees the more advanced developmental issue of the oedipus complex and other intervening developmental issues related to personal autonomy, independence, and insightful initiative. And we do expect that the by-product of thus re-living the crises of childhood growth with the more mature equipment of adolescence will be a deepened quality of self-acceptance in the individuals who participate in this experience.

By the fifth meeting there are increasing references to individuality followed by the first frank ventilation of unconscious material within the automatic safety of dream descriptions:

**G:** Do you tend to drift away from your parents as you grow older?

**G:** When I get out of this class my mind is a blank.

**G:** What makes things in your past that you had forgotten all of a sudden come out?

**G:** Will things that don't bother us now, or never bothered us before, bother us later because of these meetings?

(The group's transference of omnipotence onto the leader is now not much more than a gesture that permits these concerns to be phrased as questions. They are not felt so much as information-seeking questions as they are anxiety-reducing questions.)

**G:** I was out with an older boy. He noticed and remembered everything I said and did. It made me feel spied on.

**L:** If we notice you, listen to you, pay attention to you, remember what you say, why are we doing it?

**G:** We're apt to have another fight in here and we don't want to give out ammunition by getting into anything controversial.

**G:** Can we talk about dreams?

(La. describes a dream in which An. had three baby boys and was pregnant again. She wanted a girl very badly and she had a girl.

Po. dreamt of her sister. "She was going to have a baby. She was coming from a long distance (something about induced labor). All of a sudden she is walking along and the baby drops out, and it wasn't due yet. I saw her pick it up and put it back in again. It wasn't due. I couldn't understand why it would come out when it wasn't due yet.")

**G:** My mother dreamt that two particular people would die and they did the very next week.

**L:** You might be thinking about what these dreams can tell us; about what is going on behind the scenes. In the next class period I'll tell you something of how dreams work.

(The rest of this meeting is spent discussing the pros and cons of belonging to a group and the relative merits of "lonely individuality." The resistance takes the form of complaints that "in this group we're all *put* together. It isn't like with chosen friends." The meeting ends re-examining the confidentiality clause.)

Prior to the sixth meeting much resistance to the agreement had taken the form of loyalty to family members "who aren't here to protect themselves." However, with the imminence of transferring the oedipal conflict onto the group's relationship with the leader and the greater threat that this represented, the group in the sixth and seventh meetings entered a period of catharsis in respect to previously unexpressed negative feelings toward their parents— this after first coming to grips once again with the issue of the group's trustworthiness.

**L:** It's a little frightening, isn't it, to think of ourselves as someone others want to respect and depend on?

(Group discusses what "maturity" means.)

**G:** Compared to you (leader) we aren't mature about psychology.
(Silence)

**G:** In other words the question is: Am I mature enough to listen to other persons' problems; to have the responsibility of knowing?

**G:** I think we're afraid we're going to hurt someone in the group.

(Silence)

**G:** I know someone who knows me very well. She is an older person. Everything is O.K. between us as long as it's impersonal, but as soon as it comes to a personal problem you can't confront her with it.

**G:** Why is it parents sometimes give material things but nothing else?

**G:** They're showing their love through giving things.

**G:** Maybe they don't know how to really show their love and they give presents to keep from feeling guilty.

**G:** But sometimes tangible things aren't enough.

**G:** I'd rather be poor in a family that showed their love than have to settle for Cadillacs and for trips to Europe.
(The group is keeping all this in the third person but it is obvious to all that they are referring to their own families.)

**G:** How can you tell a person that material things are not enough?

(The group goes along with the third person reference, until one member makes a direct personal confrontation to another.)

**G:** Maybe you're afraid to show *your* love. *Your love!* Is it your mother you're talking about?

**G:** Yes.

**G:** I have the same problem with my father. He'll give me anything I want but it isn't enough. I can't get close to him. If I try it's like I've committed a crime and he sends me to my room like a child.

**G:** I can get close to my mother when it comes to just general family problems, but as soon as it gets below the surface with something that really bothers me I can't talk to her. She doesn't have the power to understand me.

(This continues more and more intensely through the meeting and ends on a new note of group intimacy.)

**G:** When my mother cuts me off with that business of my being too young when it's obvious that she's the one who can't take it I could scream!

**G:** And you know things you know they don't think you know and you want to tell them and you can't. I don't think my father would believe I knew where babies came from unless I had one to prove it!

**L:** We've seen that *we* made some assumptions when we were little that don't hold up any more. Is it possible that parents too can have assumptions that are out of date?

**G:** Yes!

**G:** How can we tell them this?

**G:** How can we get them to look at their assumptions?

**L:** How do we do it here?

**G:** Talk it out.

**G:** Here it's different. We can realize our blind spots because we're not afraid to.

**G:** It's funny. You never realize. I thought I was the only one with a problem like mine with my mother.

**G:** Me too. I feel like a weight has been lifted off me.

**G:** I feel like celebrating.

(The meeting ends with consensus on the fact that "It's our sexual things that are hardest on parents.")

By the ninth meeting the group had grown sufficiently strong to express openly its negative transference toward the leader. The meeting began with reference to a father who encourages phone calls and then "refuses to accept the charges."

**L:** So if a person in authority acts one way one time and another way another time it makes for confusion.

**G:** (sarcastically) Now *that* was a brilliant deduction!

**L:** Have you noticed that my behavior is different in the class periods from what it is here in the groups?

**G:** You're a teacher in the class. In the group you're just here.

**G:** You're part of the group. Sometimes not even that. Just extra baggage. There (class) you're top man.

**G:** We're used to it now because we know what to expect.

**G:** Don't change now. It would take another three months to get used to it.

**L:** What *is* my role in the group?

**G:** You're a moderator.

**G:** You ask leading questions.

**G:** You keep us from using our fronts.

**L:** Is this what you want from me?

**G:** I wish you'd give your opinions more than you do.

**G:** Me too. I think you must be an introvert or something.

**G:** You're thinking about us all the time but you never say what you think of us. You just sit there and listen all the time.

**G:** He does the class discussions from what we say here.

**L:** Is this what you meant by my being extra baggage?

**G:** Yes, I think you should talk more.

**G:** I think maybe you're afraid to incriminate yourself because you don't want to have hard feelings toward us. I mean you don't want us to have hard feelings toward you.

(The slip betrays the group's projections of its fears. Let's see where it leads.)

**L:** Do you mean I may be afraid of being disliked?

**G:** I mean we have to be here together the rest of the year, and you have to too.

**L:** There certainly does seem to be strong pressure to keep everything nice. What happens when we don't *feel* that way?

**G:** Nobody says a word.

**G:** Well why don't we do something about it? We all recognize it, myself included.

**G:** I think you respect someone's ideas more if you know they are telling you the truth even if it hurts.

**G:** What do the rest of you think? Is Mr. J. afraid to say what he thinks of us because he has to live with us for the rest of the year?

**G:** Maybe we're not afraid. Maybe we don't dislike you. Maybe we like you, did you ever think of that?

**G:** Mr. J., you must have an inferiority complex. Do you *want* us to hate you?

**G:** You probably have a reason for not giving us your opinions. What is it?

(Silence)

**G:** He won't answer questions. He never has once.

**G:** We've said everything there is to say without your answering. There is no more.

**L:** I think as we go along more will come.

**G:** That's the neatest trick; to just sit there and reflect questions! You don't have to say anything. You're all powerful!

**G:** You (leader) always get others to answer for you.

**G:** You're obnoxious.

**G:** What is your reason for not answering?

**G:** We had it all figured out that you were part of this group, so you ought to be one of us.

**G:** But then he could come up with *all* the answers.

**G:** You start us analyzing too soon. It kills the discussion.

**L:** What do you think the answer is?

**G:** You want us to discover things for ourselves. Well, that's fine, but when we hit the rough spots we need you.

**G:** I'll tell you how I feel when you don't answer. You're just being rude, so there!

**G:** Look at him. He just sits there grinning like a cheshire cat.

**G:** Look, he's blushing!

**L:** Feelings have a way of getting expressed one way or another, don't they?

**G:** Yes, but because you blushed doesn't give us the answer.

**G:** What embarrassed you so?

**G:** I don't see why you should be afraid. You're here to help us. Maybe you're afraid we won't be frank with you about ourselves.

**L:** And you're not paying me to be afraid, are you?

**G:** We? Paying you?

**G:** He's trying to get out of it.
(The group continues to disagree on whether or not the leader is afraid.)

**G:** He's answered by his actions.

**G:** This doesn't apply just to Mr. J. but to everyone here.

L: It is human nature for the younger person to be afraid when he sees that the older person is afraid. Now if I am afraid of being disliked then what can you do with the inevitable times when you do dislike me for a while? As you can plainly see I *do* have feelings. Whether being afraid of being disliked is one of these you'll have to find out in ways that will come to you as we go along. In any event I'm sure you are going to feel un-nicely toward me from time to time and I'm also sure that it is bad for you to keep that to yourself, because then you can only feel un-nicely toward yourself and not know why.

G: But you're *not* afraid? *Are* you?

G: He's only afraid of what would defeat the purpose of this class. We're just a pet project of his.

G: Everyone is afraid to say certain things.

G: No one can say *every*thing they feel.

L: We have lots of time.

In the tenth meeting the group plunges headlong into the oedipal conflict in all of the complex vicissitudes of sexual desire, sexual defeat and consequent despair that typifies this developmental crisis.

(The meeting began with references to "something holding us back"; to everyone's "not being frank enough"; and then to how hard it was to change over from the patterns of everyday living to "this." This was followed by many silences, fidgeting, and what the group had come to refer to as its "scatterbrain front," i.e., breaking up into small sub-groups, all talking at once. There seemed also to be an unusually intense bitterness in the group's usually playful mockery of the leader's sobriety. Then:)

G: We're having fun and not doing what we're supposed to.

G: This is our vacation self.

L: I don't think you're having fun.

G: Oh, I suppose we're avoiding something!

G: You know what I think is missing here? A sense of humor.

G: You don't think we're enjoying this?

L: Not completely.

G: Why?

L: Because people only really enjoy each other when they're doing together what they've agreed to do together.

**G:** It doesn't help with you (leader) questioning all the time and saying we're scared.

**G:** We could all bring something up. We all have problems. Maybe we *need* to scatterbrain it for a while to let them come up.

**L:** You're right. They can't be forced.

(This is followed by a deliberately whimsical discussion of what the members had for breakfast.)

**G:** What did *you* (leader) have for breakfast?

(The leader is prepared to answer these questions but follows his custom of answering only to a unified group.)

**G:** What are *you* (leader) doing over the vacation!

**G:** I'm sorry! How stupid of me to ask *you* a question!

(Sulks)

**L:** Why didn't I answer?

**G:** Maybe you don't know.

**L:** I know.

**G:** Maybe he thinks it's none of our business.

**G:** He's not giving away anything he's doing over vacation, so there!

(It finally gets across that answers cannot be given over the "scatterbrain front.")

**G:** All right. Everyone listen and now you (leader) answer.

(The technique employed to the end of facilitating a realistic re-living of the oedipal struggle was to answer all personal questions short of frankly sexual ones as candidly as possible, while simultaneously conveying by references to the agreement and by other illustrations of "the analytic attitude" that the leader was out of bounds as a sexual object.)

**G:** What are you (leader) doing over the vacation?

**L:** (answer)

**G:** Are you different outside the group?

**L:** Do you mean what kind of a person might I be *in* the group?

**G:** Do you analyze everything when you're not working?

**L:** (answer)

**G:** Do you drink; smoke; go to parties?

**L:** (answers)

**L:** Do you notice anything that your questions have in common?

(Facial expressions indicate a definite awareness of the sexual implications.)

**G:** You probably like wild life.

**G:** Your hobby is probably deep-sea diving.

**G:** What sports do you like?

**L:** (answer)

**G:** Do you live alone?

**L:** Why do you want to know?

**G:** Maybe we want to analyze you and see what you are like.

**G:** Maybe we think you're being too personal with us.

**G:** Are you married?

**L:** (answer)

**G:** Do you like children?

**G:** He likes us.

**G:** Were you close to your parents?

**L:** (answer)

**G:** Were you an only child?

**L:** (answer)

**G:** Do you like being a psychologist?

**L:** (answer)

**G:** How much do you get paid?

**L:** (answer)

**G:** I think teachers ought to be paid more.

**G:** What's the difference between a psychiatrist and a psychologist?

**L:** I would like to refer that question to the next class meeting.

**G:** Did you rebel too when you were our age?

**G:** What were you like as a child?

**G:** Has the other class asked you these things?

**L:** As you know I cannot answer that without breaking my agreement with the others, but I can say that these are natural and necessary questions because empty spaces between people are felt as dangerous until we find out what is inside them, then they are neither empty nor dangerous.

**G:** Could we help you with your problems?

**G:** We don't have the experience.

**G:** You haven't answered. Could we help you (leader) with your problems?

**L:** Yes.

**G:** We might happen to say something that would unconsciously help, and he might not realize it until later.

**G:** It depends on his bringing up a personal problem of his own.

**G:** I think what really matters is that he thinks we *could* help. He isn't really going to bring his own up.

**L:** Any time I can bring in my own experience in a way that seems helpful I shall. I will not bring up personal problems because it is not in our agreement. It would be an unnecessary burden to you.

(Silence)

**G:** This meeting reminds me of a dream I had last night.

(The dream is as follows: The school was like a palace in looks. All the steps in the school were white marble. There were glass enclosed wings which came out on either side of the main building. When you stood facing the front of the building the glass enclosure on the left was the psychology room. Beyond the terrace was a hill with steps leading downward and a path just at the bottom which led into nowhere. It just faded into nowhere.

Well, one day after school I came into your (leader's) room and asked you if I could come for a conference the next day. You said yes, at any time. I replied, "Is after school at 2:30 all right?" You answered "Yes." The next day I walked in to talk to you but you seemed to have changed. I started to open my mouth to say something when you said, "What are you doing here, I don't want to see you, go on out of here." I was somewhat shocked and told you that you said I could come at that time, but you still insisted that you were right. Then you got up and walked out on the terrace to the fountain where you stood with one leg up on a higher step than the other and your head resting on your hand. You were talking to some of the women teachers and seemed to be quite happy with life. I never could see the faces of the teachers. I stood down below and kept saying, "But Mr. Jones, you promised." Then you began to bawl me out. You said, "Will you please go away, I don't know what you are talking about. Now will you please go." I replied with the same "But you promised me." You said to the teachers, "Just pay no attention to her, I don't know what she's talking about. I don't even know her." I then repeated the same line about six times. Just before you came down from the steps you said, "My good child, will you leave me alone." Then you came down from the steps, went down the hill and began to run down the path that led to nowhere. I took out after you saying "Mr. Jones, you promised me." Then all of a sudden I sat up in bed. To tell you the truth I thought it was real.)

**L:** What do you make of the dream?

**G:** I have absolutely no idea why I dreamt this or no idea what it may mean, although last night I was thinking about it, and I wondered if it could symbolize the smoking problem between me and my father. Maybe you were taking the place of him, and I was trying to get the truth out of him on the problem.

**G:** What do you think the dream means, Sir?
   (This is the first time the leader has been referred to in such a formal way.)

**L:** The dream seems to feel that women aren't worth giving faces to, and that the man has all the answers.

**G:** It makes you (leader) more human just to know you *have* problems.

**L:** How would (absent member) have felt about this meeting?
   (This evolves into a discussion of the importance of all the members being present.)

**G:** It might not feel important but we'd realize the difference if anyone dropped out.

**G:** Who gets the most out of these meetings, the ones who talk or the ones who don't?
   (Silence)

**G:** Why don't you answer my question!

**G:** He wants to leave a cavity (sic).
   (At this point the group's associations take on a markedly regressed flavor.)

**G:** Look, it's snowing out.

**G:** Let's go out and build an igloo.

**G:** Can we all go out and throw snowballs?

**G:** Can we have a party next week?

**G:** Sir, why did you change the subject from you to us?

**L:** I think I can still be useful to you.

**G:** You weren't kidding when you said self-knowledge wasn't easy.

**G:** I hate myself.

**G:** What makes a person want to commit suicide?

**G:** Yes, tell us that in the next class meeting.

**G:** The other day I almost ran in front of a truck. I just thought "what would it feel like?"

**G:** Why you want to commit suicide is probably when you get so mad at your parents you really feel just frustrated.

**G:** It's probably that you feel like killing *them.*

(From this meeting on the leader was addressed as "Sir." This form of address came to communicate a remarkable blend of meanings. It semed to simultaneously convey respect, distance, affection, resentment, and most of all, control over the keeping of distance.)

If there were any doubt concerning the direct relationships of this meeting to the oedipal experiences of childhood they were dispelled at the next meeting which opened as follows:

**G:** Sir, can I ask something? It's awfully embarrassing! What does it mean when you dream that you married your father? I'm scared to death it might mean something horrible.

(The dream was as follows: Well, it seems that my father didn't think I was going to marry. He didn't want me to marry or something. I can't remember what the reason was. Anyway, he told me that he and I were going to be married and that everything had been arranged and that there was nothing to worry about. The scene was then changed to a hotel in someplace but yet no place. All there was was a room on the tenth floor hanging in space. In the room were twin beds which we pushed together and in them were to sleep my mother, two sisters, father and myself. I apparently thought the whole set-up was quite odd and asked just what was going on. I asked my mother if she was sure she wanted to divorce daddy so he could marry me. She replied that everything was O.K. and not to worry. I then asked daddy when we were to be married and he replied not for three weeks and we were going to have our honeymoon first so I could see how I liked married life. I remember I was completely confused but thought I'd better go along with my parents because I was afraid of being punished if I didn't. I remember also that there was a look in both mother's and daddy's eye which placed a fear inside of me.

When it came time to go to bed I was to sleep between daddy and mother. I was completely petrified. Morning came, I guess, since the next thing I remember was afternoon. Now this is the real odd thing. We were then in the basement of a school I used to go to. Beside this was a wide river of nothing but quicksand and on the other side of this was England, and a beautiful castle was just the other side of the quicksand. Do you follow me?

Well, there was some sort of an exhibit there and that was the reason for our presence. The next thing I recall was my running down the hall of the basement just as fast as I could go and a girl grabbed my arm as I ran by. She said that she knew why I was running and that she was in the same boat, so we continued running together. It seems that the reason for my running was because I decided that my parents were just trying to make a fool out of me and then there was something about a baby involved but I don't know what it was. It also seems that this girl had the same exact trouble only the male involved was young and named Bill. We ran out the door which had the quicksand in front of it and I said that if we could get across it we'd be O.K. This girl said that we couldn't but I insisted, so we proceeded to cross. I said that if you gave a running start and kept running all the way across you'd make it. So across we went. I remember it was harder for her to cross than it was for me. We both lost our shoes as they stuck in the sand while crossing. Then I woke up.)

The rest of this meeting was summarized in the minutes as follows:

La. said that she had been having strange dreams lately too. Ba. said that she didn't want to marry her father. It was told to the group that there was a girl at school whose father was also her stepbrother. After a discussion of how this could be true, there was a great silence. That day all the girls who took Civics had to invest money in the stock exchange and that was our next topic. Everyone told how much money they had received from their stocks (mistyped sticks). Silence again . . . It was asked if bedwetting was a sign of confusion about sex. I think that Mr. J. said that a lot of things could point out a confusion about sex and didn't everyone feel this confusion when they were little and even now?

An. referred back to the dream that Ba. brought up and said that maybe it meant that she didn't want to marry her father but wanted to be more like him. La. said that she'd rather be like her mother. Ba. said just the opposite. Silence . . .

Other subjects which seemed minor but filled up the time were:
Someone in the kitchen was on an egg diet.
Dates for this week-end.
The glee club concerts.
Saltpeter and what its effect is on a person.

Po. asked why we were so interested in sex? Some of the reasons given were:

It is hard to find out about.
There is such a confusion that people want to know more about it.
It is also hard because of the sophisticated front you have to put on. You also wouldn't have the confidence to bring some questions about sex up. A hazard might be that you felt alone in your feelings and might feel foolish. Ga. said that you might want to tell a problem but not be able to. Why can a person get depressed from a daydream? One reason given was daydreams get inside of your feelings and bring them into reality. I think that Mr. J. went back to what Ga. had said and repeated the idea of wanting to say something but couldn't. We have feelings that we have to fight inside ourselves and also feelings that we don't feel comfortable with. Then we talked about the problem of always bringing up the subject of sex in class and why we

did. We know a lot but we are not sure. We haven't too much experience about it. We also wonder if it is right to have certain feelings.

It becomes clear in the meeting that with the reassurance of the leader's support in guiding sexual impulses away from the incestuous object, namely himself as the parent figure, the group is now ready to tolerate the higher level derivatives of its sexual impulses that had formerly been inhibited, namely, sexual curiosity and information seeking. This freedom to verbalize its sexual interests on an intellectual plane continued throughout the course of the group's development but was largely confined to the class meetings where the leader's answering of questions did not have the unconscious connotations that it had in the group meetings.

However, the unconscious interpretations of the oedipal defeat, namely the fantasy of having been castrated (losing the shoes in the quicksand) as a consequence of having harbored the incestuous wish, had now become intensified. This became manifest in the group's consciousness by heightened feelings of worthlessness, emptiness, and failure; and by a resultant new wave of hostility toward the leader, now even more dangerous in that it sought to destroy the very force which the group needed in order to keep the incestuous wish in check. There was an interesting linguistic subtlety that arose in the group at this time that seemed to reflect how the forces of the transference handled this exigency. The leader as "Sir" seemed to be perceived still as the permissive but limit-setting figure who was now safely, though still somewhat reluctantly, taboo as a sexual object. He became the respected sanctioner of sexual feelings but the prohibitor of their incestuous direction. "Sir," therefore, remained an ally of the ego. "Psychology," however, and therefore the leader as psychologist, became the castrating parent which "cuts the life out of us" and became the object of the group's unconscious rage in respect to its feelings of loss. "Psychology," therefore, became the symbol of the infantile superego while "Sir" as the mature conscience was left free to aid the ego in its reorganizing efforts.

Thus the author in seeking to facilitate psychological growth in depth found himself in the ironic position of a psychology teacher entering an emotional alliance against his own subject!

The thirteenth and fourteenth meetings represented the critical period with respect to facing the castration fantasy, or rather the conscious and pre-conscious derivatives of the castration fantasy. The leader's aims were to facilitate the outward expression of the hostility and to subtly encourage the search for a more realistic model of feminine adequacy than the fantasied lost one.

(The reader of the minutes began the thirteenth meeting by deprecating her contribution because "I left out a lot." The group recalls several omitted items.)

**G:** Did I leave anything else out? *I'm sure something is missing.*

(The topic shifts to daydreams and wishful thinking as "a way of getting away from uncomfortable feelings.")

**G:** (a member who had discovered Freud's Introductory Lectures) I think "psychology" puts too much emphasis on father images and childhood. Shouldn't we be thinking more in terms of husband-images nowadays?

**G:** Take The Prophet (on the reading list). Psychology can *tear it apart*, but it's pure poetry and ought to be enjoyed—*not dissected.*

**G:** Psychology seems to explain everything away. It doesn't *leave much of anything*. It's so materialistic and narrow. It doesn't leave room for dignity. That isn't what I mean. That doesn't sound right now. I'm not as upset now as I was before.

**L:** I don't understand.

**G:** Well, there is something vicious that's been going on in this class and I can't put my finger on it. Psychology is so easy to take as a symbol of whatever it is that is wrecking everything.

(Group expresses confusion.)

**G:** I think I understand what you mean. I've been feeling it too. Something doesn't feel right.

**L:** What?

**G:** Well, I'd hate to think that the greatest piece of art is only a compulsive expression of somebody's unconscious.

**L:** Not worth anything in its own right.

**G:** Psychology seems to say "Well, here you are. *Everything is inside of you* and everything you do comes from yourself and what you've been made."

**G:** I think you came here looking for the complete answer and you haven't found it so you're disappointed.

(The topic shifts to the psychoanalytic interpretation of Hamlet.)

**L:** Why does it tear Hamlet apart to see the unconscious side of it?

**G:** Well, *psychology makes everything so empty. There's nothing in you.* It doesn't give you any personality. It always *leaves something missing.* I don't know, Sir, you've probably confronted this before too, and can say it better.

**L:** Does it have anything to do with your complaint that I am only here to observe you as objects of experimental study?

(This develops into a speculative discussion of the leader's motives for teaching in a girls' school.)

**G:** Psychologists have to create an illusion of interest in the people they see.

**G:** You (leader) may be just interested in us out of curiosity.

**L:** And it may be idle curiosity?

**G:** Yes, cause we don't know if you're absolutely interested in us or not cause you just sit there.

**G:** Like when Ga. was saying that she wants to bring things up but can't. You weren't interested in her, you were only interested in why she couldn't.

**G:** It's not a compliment to be seen as objects.

**G:** I might feel accepted and comfortable as an object to you (leader)—as just another person you'll meet as a psychologist.

**L:** Yes, you could get used to just being an object.

**G:** I think that is easier to adjust to than that you (leader) have a personal interest in each one of us.

**L:** I'm sure it is.

**G:** I mean you *have to be.* If you start developing a personal interest in each one of us, oh, you're going to get in a mess.

**L:** Do you have to protect me from this mess?

**G:** No, if you become personally interested in me what can I do about it? It's just that if I were in your position I wouldn't because then you wouldn't be dealing with psychology any more.

**G:** I certainly hope you (leader) do have feelings. You'd be a pretty blah person otherwise. Excuse me, Sir. But I think you realize you can't bring your own personal feelings into it unless you can express it like a psychologist.

(This frank expression of the group's need of super-ego support from the leader is in contrast to the frequent manifestation of resistance in the form of complaining about the leader's objectivity and passivity.)

**G:** I'm getting worn out!

**G:** Do you (leader) think I'm getting worried because psychology doesn't treat us as human beings?

**L:** You say there is something missing.

**G:** Do you (leader) expect us to completely open up?

**G:** You (leader) bother me. I remember you once saying "There must be something dangerous" and it made me mad. I could have thrown something at you.

**G:** It's like being tested.

**G:** Do you really expect us to let all barriers down and feel perfectly free as the breeze? That's stupid. You act as if there isn't anything we couldn't say or do, and you don't give us credit for trying our best at a very difficult thing. It gives me a very weird feeling.

**G:** You (leader) expect us to sit here and spiel off down to our insides. It rubs me the wrong way. It's like you are saying there's something wrong with me, that I should feel guilty about something, and I don't like it. I mean I don't like it thrown in my face that way.

**L:** Certainly not by someone who treats you as an empty object in the first place.

**G:** Yes! (brushing back tears)

**L:** I know very well how difficult a thing you're all trying to do here and I know how hard you're searching, but yes, I do expect you to *go on* searching.

G: But we could go on talking till the leaves turn blue and it wouldn't change things.

G: It's this feeling of being on trial that I don't like.

L: And by someone who has pre-judged you as being lacking.

G: It's *you*, Sir! It's especially *you*. If another teacher said it it wouldn't bother me a bit. They don't know the real me, but you do if anyone does, and when *you* say something is missing I feel completely defeated.

L: When I say there is something missing I am simply repeating what I've heard *you* say.

G: I'll tell you the danger I feel in here. If I'm completely honest, I'm going to hurt somebody. It's happened before.

L: This, I'm sure, is why I feel so protected in here.

G: But you don't usually come right out and say you think a person is an idiot or he's pretty nice.

G: Especially not to a teacher.

G: You usually respect a person because he's a teacher and that's as far as it goes.

G: You show your respect by not showing your feelings.

L: Do you mean you have to choose between having dignity and having feelings?

G: Sometimes it's impossible to show your feelings.

L: Isn't that why we made our agreement?

G: I don't see where all this is getting.

G: I don't see where it's coming from.

L: It's coming from you.

The fourteenth meeting shows a continued handling of the castration fantasy. It also contains foreshadowings of the type of resistance to be employed in the working through period that was to follow.

(The group began this meeting in a pointedly disinterested mood with the majority of the members occupied in reading, knitting, letter writing, etc. It was if they were saying, "We are here because we have to be. We don't like it, but we will go through the motions of a meeting." One member attempted to recall the main theme of the previous meeting but was unsuccessful amid the group's attempts to turn the meeting into a classroom situation. For example, "What is the chemical formula

for sugar?" The leader's premature attempt to focus the meeting on the unresolved issue of the previous meeting was met
with:)

**G:** You (leader) do that every week, sir, and we never get anywhere with it.

**G:** If you ask me there is something missing in this whole idea of
a group.

**L:** Why has the paraphernalia of the school room suddenly become more important than the people in it?

**G:** *We don't want to look at ourselves.*

**G:** We're busy. I have to finish my biology assignment.

(The group discusses cutting up animals in the biology lab.)

**G:** Last week you (leader) were trying to make us say that what
was lacking was we felt we were being looked at as objects instead of people. I don't think so because I think we *are* being
looked at as people and there is *still* something missing.

**G:** I don't think we're accomplishing anything.

**G:** I agree.

**G:** I don't think we've accomplished anything all year—anything
really important.

**G:** The main thing I've gotten in this course is that it has made me
appreciate the other ones more by contrast.

**G:** But if we can't do something in this course it must show we're
pretty young.

**G:** Right!

**G:** I used to enjoy these meetings until we started talking about
something missing. Then I got an uncomfortable feeling and I
started worrying.

**G:** We get more out of the class meetings than these group meetings.

**G:** These seem to be getting worse instead of better.

**G:** I think we're learning that we can be discouraged if we're not
kept interested all the time.

**L:** You would prefer to be getting something you're not?

**G:** Yes.

**L:** What?

**G:** It would be better if we sat around that table all the time and not just in the class meetings.

**G:** Sir, do you have an extra blue book you can lend me?

(Silence, followed by a disorganized discussion of knitting, vacation matters and recent dreams.)

**G:** Sir, what does it mean when you dream in color?

(Leader refers this to a class meeting.)

**G:** Why not now? We'd get so much further that way. Here we are asking for help and you don't give it. I don't understand that.

**G:** We're trying and you (leader) won't help.

**G:** He doesn't want us to think he knows all about us.

**G:** Are you (leader) really interested in us?

**L:** Yes.

**G:** How do you mean, one of us or all of us?

**L:** All.

**G:** But you're not interested in our technicolor dreams.

(Silence.)

**G:** Don't you (leader) have anything in your life *but* psychology?

**G:** Do you have any life of your own?

**G:** You're the only person in this class who doesn't wander the way we do. The only person who keeps us on a line.

**L:** Isn't that what you're paying me for?

**G:** No, you're not keeping the agreement.

**G:** You just sit there. You never get excited. You never get angry. We could get up and do the Highland Fling and you'd just sit there.

**G:** Don't you think if you *did* give more that what you want and what we want would finally come about?

**L:** You'll bring it about.

**G:** Do you have *any* opinions of your own?

**L:** Yes.

**G:** But they don't belong here?

**L:** I think there is something in between us here that we don't see.

**G:** Do you mean that you *and* us don't see, or just us?

**L:** Just you on this point.

**G:** *Is it that the group is a she and you're a he?*

**L:** That's certainly a difference, isn't it?

**G:** Sir, *are* you afraid of being hurt?

**G:** I think he is.

**G:** I bet you( leader) are almost the same outside as you are here. I just wonder how you've developed the ability to sit there with your hands folded and that calm expression and say "yes" and "uh-huh." I think it's a defense.

**G:** Do you (leader) really hear what we say?

**L:** Yes.

**G:** It must go in one ear and out the other.

**G:** Oh, he takes us seriously.

**G:** I don't think he does.

**G:** I do.

**G:** There is nothing unpredictable about him.

**G:** I don't think there is any doubt that we *trust* him. It's more that we don't *know* him.

**G:** Sir, maybe we *are* getting to know you. Maybe you're *not* different outside.

**L:** I don't feel as protected outside as I do here.

**G:** Is it protecting you to say I don't think much of your course?

**G:** If you're a machine then we can kick you, but when you know a person you know what you can say to them and what their reactions will be. But *you* never show any reactions.

**L:** I don't really believe that. You've seen many of my reactions as I well remember.

**G:** You know, you're making me feel like right now I don't care what I say to you. Excuse me, but damn it, it shouldn't be that way. I could tell you to go jump off a pier!

**L:** Is that because of our agreement or because you feel I'm not interested anyway?

**G:** I don't think you care what I say to you!

**G:** I'm beginning to feel the same way.

**G:** You've just deflated everything.

**G:** I feel completely uninhibited now and in a few minutes the bell is going to ring and I have to go to a class where it's Yes Ma'am —No Ma'am and put yourself on report if you breathe the wrong way, and that's not good for me. Psychology is supposed to help you think better. When I leave here I can't think at all for two hours. Can you sit there and say that is good for me?

**L:** I can't honestly say it's bad for you.

**G:** Why?

**L:** Thinking isn't everything.

(Bell)

**L:** I think we're reaching the point where we might begin to think about friendship and whether it is better to build a friendship on the basis of what each *lacks* or on what each *has*.

The group was now to begin a process of working through its anxiety in respect to independent femininity that was to carry it through the next nine meetings. These meetings were characterized by marked evidences of regression and anticipatory progression in the group's associations, of regression in its choice of defenses and of firm maintenance in the transference of the independent separateness that it had derived from the oedipal defeat, and had partially consolidated in its initial facing of its castration anxieties. The furniture was to take on no little symbolic meaning in this period, with the seminar table symbolizing both the securities of pre-genital dependence and the group's autonomy in relation to the parent-leader, while it also seemed to serve as a manipulable, protective shield against the castrating leader. The open circle came to function somewhat as a screen memory that condensed both the traumata and the unfilled promises of the oedipal period.

In the class meeting immediately following the fifteenth group meeting the group unanimously decided to discontinue holding its group meetings in the open circle and to hold them instead around the classroom table. The leader abstained from the voting, but kept the issue open by continuing to prepare the room for open circle meetings on the days of the group meetings. Consequently, at each group meeting the group was confronted with the physical evidence of *choice*. The leader's technique throughout this period was to permit and often to actively support the regression, while at the same time interpreting it, at first very mildly and later very directly, and also while communicating in many non-verbal ways his expectation that the group would choose to return to the circle.

The seventeenth meeting marked the high point in the regressive aspects of the group's reorganizing efforts. The meeting was predominated by vigorous and open-styled assertions of self and exaggerated experimentation with grown up mannerisms—all behind a depersonalizing screen of comfortably indulged playfulness. There was in all of this a marked flavor of womanliness. The leader's picture was of a group of girls romping together in their mothers' shoes, dresses, and mannerisms.

(The meeting began with the group questioning the leader's motives in continuing to set up the tape recorder and the open circle and asking if the other group had their group meetings in a circle.)

**G:** Now children, you must pay attention to our little minutes!

**G:** Let's have a big argument.

**G:** Now children!

**G:** I hate you.

**G:** You are being just as rude as you can be.

**G:** It's a wonderful world!

**G:** Psychology is trying to break it up.

**G:** Let's have a big fight.

**G:** This whole group is extremely rude.

**G:** Mary had a little lamb . . .

**G:** Mr. J., get La. to tell you about her date last weekend.

**G.** Will you get mad, Sir, if I tell a risque joke?

**G:** Go ahead. Let's hear it.

(The punch line refers to a "pearl-handled gun for formal weddings.")

(The group grows more and more boisterous with members having to shout to make themselves heard.)

**G:** Stop moving the table!

(References to "sexy stories," "underclothes," "locking the door against Yale men.")

**G:** Sir, why don't you come down and join us?

**G:** Who would keep the group on its course if he did?

**G:** What course?

**G:** Yes, where are we going?

(Then, in an uncanny manner that has to be imagined, four members spontaneously lapsed into a kind of sing-song meter:)

**G:** The group is going on the straight and narrow.

**G:** To where we don't know.

**G:** Reminds me of Pilgrim's Progress. Sir, do you think that's a good book for us to be reading now?

**G:** We're walking through the valley of the shadow of death.

**G:** And the snakes are everywhere.

**G:** You should read *"Farewell to Arms."* It's tremendous.

**G:** Let's go out and have a snowball fight.

**G:** Let's go swing on the swings.

**G:** (from under the table) Sir, you should look at the group from this angle.

**G:** Let's go outside and have a smoke.

**G:** Let's have ice cream next time.

(One member takes down what flavor each wants and meets silence when she asks the leader his favorite flavor, at which the tension in the group nears panic.)

**L:** The rule of the group is *as long as you put it in words*, anything goes.

**G:** You (leader) are not being consistent.

(This objection is very mild and the tension decreases.)

**G:** Mr. J., do you think we're accomplishing anything?

**L:** Are you learning the value of play?

(This is briefly discussed.)

**L:** You see, much can be discovered in play that can't be in more serious moods. What are you discovering?

**G:** We're knowing each other in different ways.

**G:** Can't play be dangerous?

**L:** The only danger is not knowing where to stop, or, when you're little, not having anyone to stop you.

(The discussion turns to how two absent members would have behaved in this meeting.)

**G:** Ba. would have gotten annoyed. She gets nervous and her skin breaks out, especially around boys.

**G:** Na. takes this group very seriously. She gets bothered when we mention something being missing.

**L:** Have you ever wondered what is *not* missing?

**G:** You (leader) tell us.

**L:** You are perfectly equipped for that.

**G:** Mr. J., that won't work. Why don't you try it our way?

**L:** And your way is?

**G:** You answering our questions.

The eighteenth meeting was marked by an intensification of the group's exclusion of the leader

**G:** We don't care about you (leader).

**G:** You aren't important any more.

**G:** We like the group better than you.

In the nineteenth meeting the issue of the group's personal autonomy, which had, of course, been present from the beginning, began to crystallize into the form in which it was to be resolved—such as it was resolved. The table began to symbolize on the one hand the group's power to exercise its choice, and to make it stick; on the other hand, it was beginning to become causally associated with the feeling of childishness and lack of mature accomplishment. The leader chose this meeting to confront the group with both sides of its dilemma by reassuring it of its power to continue using its essentially obsessive-compulsive defenses while at the same time referring to these defenses (via the symbol of the table) as a barrier against discovering new ways of knowing itself.

(The first half of the meeting consisted of a lethargic kind of effortful small talk with occasional expressions of dissatisfaction with "not getting anywhere.")

**L:** O.K., quiet down for a minute. You have the power to make your meetings run this way indefinitely, and if you need the rest of the year to be convinced of that then I can think of no better way to use the time. But it doesn't lead to where you want to go. Now, when people are not sure where they want to go, or how to get there, it sometimes helps to look back at where they've been. So let's hear from each of you how you have seen this group change.

**G:** We tried your (leader's) way. Now we're trying ours, but it's just as bad.

**G:** We've turned into a bunch of misbehaved little brats.

**G:** You (leader) want us to look at ourselves but I don't believe so much of that is good for a person.

**G:** We're playing now and I get something out of that. You can think about it afterward and see new angles.

**G:** I think the whole thing is a waste of time.

**G:** You (leader) are determined, whether you admit it or not, to make us do it your way but you don't help us.

**G:** I'm enjoying sun bathing on our life buoy (the group's term for a defense). I'll dive in again when someone else does, but not by myself. As long as we continue to make fun of anything serious, who's going to be serious?

**G:** (re. Ba. who is absent) Ba. takes these meetings seriously, and she's been helped the most.

**G:** (re. Je. who is absent) Je. complains and criticizes the most, but she's gained a lot even though she never admits it.

**G:** Last year's groups seemed to get so much out of these meetings. Why aren't we?

**L:** Why have you put a barrier between us?

**G:** Oh, you and that table! I'd like to put a bomb under it and blow it to pieces!

The twentieth meeting, continuing in this vein, was distinguished by a strong expression of guilt feelings and by longings for the external controls of the past. The leader continued to confront the group with its resistance to exploring new ways via the symbol of the table.

The twenty-first meeting was marked by indications of a growing sense of realistic independence and self-direction in the group. There were also signs of a new kind of awareness of the forces that work against the development of independence.

(One member who had never taken the initiative in the group's discussion until the retreat behind the table, but who had blossomed into one of its most active members since that time, set

the tone of this meeting by describing the increasing friction
between her and her mother whom she described as "being jeal-
ous of her authority; afraid of losing it; and takes her fears out
on me." The group takes this up:)

**G:** Parents are like that. They don't like to see their children grow
up.

**G:** When you grow up you see more. Parents don't look perfect
any more. They see that, and it scares them.

**G:** The more you grow, the more you take, and take, and take.

**G:** And the more you keep things private from your parents.

**G:** You want to strike out on your own and find your own way,
but this hurts your parents who want you to be like them.

**G:** Or like they wanted to be and weren't.

**G:** I feel sorry for my parents. They have so few choices left. We
have our whole lives yet.

**G:** Parents get used to being seen as perfect.

**G:** Then you grow up and see them as they are.

In the twenty-third meeting, with the initiative furnished by the
member who had become more outgoing behind the table, the
group tentatively decided to move back to the circle the next time.

**G:** I've opened up since we moved to the table. Now I'd be curious
to see how it felt back in the circle. I vote we try it once next time.

(The group votes affirmation.)

**L:** That doesn't tell us why we moved to the table in the first
place.

**G:** I think it was because the classes are so much better, so much
more organized, and we wanted the group meetings to be more
like them.

**G:** But it didn't work out that way. What makes the classes more
organized is Mr. J. being more of a teacher.

**G:** He treats us like little girls in the class.

**G:** We're even littler in here.

**G:** But we don't *have* to be.

**L:** Do you mean there is more of the "Big Must" in the classes?

(The "Big Must" had come to be the group's term for unreasonable authority.)

**G:** Yes.

**L:** Is that why you moved then, so you could safely be little girls in the presence of the "Big Must"?

**G:** We've really made a flop of this course.

**L:** Anything but!

**G:** You think we've accomplished something?

**L:** A great deal.

**G:** What?

**L:** To feel the barriers in ourselves by feeling the walls they put between people is what we agreed to do together.

**G:** What do you mean by barriers in ourselves?

**G:** I know what he means. It's like not feeling free to stay someplace because you're not sure you can leave.

**G:** Like loving to read but hating English.

**G:** Like wanting a boy to kiss you and you know he wants to, but he's not sure that you want him to, so you end up talking about the weather.

**G:** Or like wanting him to do more, but thinking you shouldn't.

**G:** Is that what you (leader) mean?

**L:** If you move back to the circle, will it be because you don't feel free to stay at the table?

**G:** No, I'm curious.

**G:** I don't know. You didn't answer my question.

**G:** This is still ridiculous.

In the twenty-fourth meeting there are continued indications of unresolved ambivalence around the issues of dependence, autonomy, and feminine adequacy, but there are also definite signs of a new kind of relaxation and poise and of emerging self-confidence in respect to these issues that can only reflect their genuine, although of course still incomplete, re-integration. This was manifest not only in the group's associations and its organization of these into an intellectually engaging discussion, but also in the mutually respectful affection and freedom to express positive feelings that characterized the personal interaction of this meeting. The latter is all the more impressive when we note that the group had long since shown itself quite free from any compulsive need to maintain the superficial variety of social amenities. The twenty-fourth meeting is therefore presented in detail.

(The group carries out its previous decision and sits in an open circle.)

G: You got a haircut, didn't you Mr. J.? Looks nice.

(Several minutes of somewhat fidgety but closely clannish social exchange among the members)

G: Who has the minutes?

G: I was waiting for someone to ask me to read them. I'm not competing with the chit-chat, but I'll wait.

G: All right, everybody listen.

(Minutes are read.)

G: An., I hear you got in the A group.

G: So did Je.

G: Isn't that wonderful!

(The group congratulates its two "geniuses.")

G: Did you hear that Marlon Brando is dating a nineteen year old girl?

(The group discusses birthdays and the coming "open" weekend, eagerly anticipating new experiences with boys and fearing the possible loss of the weekend for disciplinary reasons.)

G: If this school ever tried to stop me from that weekend I'd blow it up.

G: I'd go anyway; if (the principal) kicked me out she'd have her own conscience to face.

G: That's right. Education doesn't all go on in school. It is time she learned that.

G: I think she realizes it, but she gets panicky and goes against her better judgment.

(References to "immature teachers" who are "silly," "fakes," "pompous."

G: What they need is a good man.

G: Oh, well, at least we'll be with boys soon.

**G:** (jokingly) Mr. J., can Paul stay with you when he comes?

**G:** Can you imagine, we're eighteen or nineteen and they're still putting those idiotic rules on us!

(A brief and somewhat hysterical period of references to sexual sophistication that would "shock" the principal "if she knew.")

(References to being unfairly treated by maternal authorities in which the group warmly supports one member who had just been "treated like a baby.")

(Discussion of the future and of the coming liberality of college life with an expression of anxiety over possible rejection by one's college choice and the need to get good grades.)

**G:** What's a good book to read for the English long paper?

**G:** I'm going to read Vanity Fair.

**G:** I'm going to try something difficult for once.

**G:** (Principal) thinks we have to be threatened into being serious and studying.

(The discussion again turns to the mother figure.)

**G:** That's all she knows. "You must develop study habits," and "You're immature."

**G:** As if *she was* mature! She knows nothing about womanly things like cooking and sewing. You'd think it was a sin to be your own sex if you listen to her.

**G:** She's an idiot.

**G:** She's a jerk.

**G:** She's a good principal, though.

**G:** You feel better when she's back of you than when she's against you.

**G:** Yes, if it doesn't cost you too much.

**G:** You have to appreciate her, though, when it comes to getting into college. They respect her opinions.

(References to dreams of graduating dresses, to getting into college, to marriage, to having babies. This merges into an anticipatory discussion of college life.)

**G:** Mr. J., do you think we're accomplishing something over here (in the circle) that we didn't over there (at the table)?

**L:** What do *you* think?

**G:** One thing I've noticed. We keep coming back again and again to the idea of a kind of battle with the authorities over us.

(The group argues over who was responsible for moving back to the circle, i.e., who dropped the defense first.)

**G:** (to the member who led the vote) You fought to get over here; I didn't.

**G:** He (leader) wanted it so I passed a vote. That's all.

**L:** Is that why you chose the circle, because *I* wanted it?

**G:** No, we wanted to see how it felt too.

**G:** Is there anyone who doesn't want to be here?

**L:** (over a certain amount of hub-bub) How does it feel?

**G:** What did he say?

**G:** I didn't hear.

**G:** Sir, why don't you ever repeat things?

**G:** I know. I was talking to a second grade teacher who has a rowdy class. She says she forces them to listen by always talking softly to them.

**G:** I've seen my sister do that with her baby. When he's crying she whispers in his ear and it works.

(One member asks the group's permission to see if an important letter from a college had arrived; gets it, looks at the leader and leaves.)

**G:** (playfully) Now let's talk about her.

**G:** I'm so excited that she got in the A group.

**G:** She deserves it. She worked awfully hard for it.

**G:** Can I leave too? I can't wait till lunch to see if I heard from Dave.

**G:** Let's all leave.

(The anxiety mounts and the group becomes noisy and disorganized.)

**G:** We're challenging Mr. J.

**G:** You (leader) get a funny look in your eyes like you're staring right through me when we act like this. It makes me nervous. I wish you'd do it to someone else. You always look at me when we get like this.

**L:** That is probably true. What do you think the look says?

**G:** I think it's when you're really angry with us, and covering it up with a smile.

**G:** Is that it?

**G:** Is it?

**L:** You're becoming very astute observers.

**G:** Let's make Mr. J. blush.

**G:** Come on, Sir, blush for us.

**G:** Oh, it isn't working.

**G:** We're getting silly.

**L:** Sure, I get mad at you sometimes, because it's true, isn't it, that the group and I have been partly at odds for some time? Haven't we been having a kind of running fight.

**G:** Yes, that's right.

(General consensus)

**G:** We're against you (leader).

**G:** No, we're *for* you.

**G:** You want us to do something we don't want to do. So just to be obstinate we're going to *not* do it.

**G:** You want us to be a group and we're going to stay a class.

**G:** We're a group.

**G:** We are not. We're a class.

**G:** *We are a group!* And if you don't think so, then will you please tell me exactly what *"class"* acts like we do?

**L:** I guess in some ways this has felt like a fight between you and me. But I think what you've been fighting *against* is being seen through by unfriendly eyes, and against the Big Must. Now I'm wondering what it is you've been fighting *for*.

**G:** What is it, a fight for power?

(The group again debates why it moved back to the circle.)

**G:** So he's (leader) won then.

**G:** Not if we moved because of what we *wanted*.

**G:** The table was a barricade. You could put an imaginary one right here in the circle and it would be the same thing.

(The discussion shifts back to the leader's ability to cover his anger and to fathers who can and cannot do this.)

**G:** I like my father, I found out.

**G:** Me too, I think I'll keep him.

**G:** Somebody make an interpretation.

**G:** No, it takes all the fun out to analyze everything.

**G:** It's fun to analyze.

**G:** But it's so artificial. It's like saying, don't be angry at me, understand me instead.

**G:** When he (leader) is angry and covers it up it just makes me *more* angry.

**G:** I know that feeling. My father does it too well.

(The group discusses having opposite feelings of love and anger toward fathers and what this means.)

**L:** Is it possible for me to get angry at you at times, and still want you to win your fight?

**G:** Everyone feels, to put it right bluntly, love and hate at the same time. I *really* think that's possible.

**L:** Is there love and hate in this group?

**G:** Yes, I really think so!

**L:** By winning, what have you won?

**G:** Nothing but chaos in another part of the room.

**G:** No, we're fighting for something else.

(The group argues whether or not it has defeated the leader.)

**G:** This is not the only class we write letters in, and read other subjects and goof off in.

**G:** But this is the only one we can do it in the open and discuss anything in.

**G:** There isn't anyone here who wouldn't prefer a nice sensible meeting with everybody listening.

**G:** Then why don't we?

**G:** So we *haven't* won anything!

**G:** Maybe we want the satisfaction of changing the past where the teacher lays down the laws. We come in here and Mr. J. doesn't lay down the laws, so we have a chance to try other ways.

**L:** It sounded a while ago like some of you have been reading some pretty heavy psychology books. But you see people stage their basic life struggles in pretty earthy forms—like tables and circles; letters and books; words and funny looks.

**G:** I'm so sick of hearing about that table I'm going to burn it some day.

**G:** Could the barrier be a lack of interest?

**G:** Where does the other group sit?

**L:** Everyone has their own kind of props.

**G:** I think we're fighting for power over you (leader) because you don't act normal and answer questions.

**G:** *Maybe we're fighting for Mr. J. to give the answers to prove that we don't have any answers ourselves, but we really do!*

**G:** We're fighting to find something we're all interested in.

**G:** We're fighting to find what we have in common.

(Silence)

**G:** You know, perhaps we're getting more out of the group than we think.

**G:** We are!

**G:** I remember you (leader) said that a long time ago. You said there was more going on underneath than we knew.

**L:** You see, I have a strong conviction that I *know* what it is you're looking for, and that is a good thing.

**G:** What is it?

**G:** We know, "do we want you to do our work for us?"

**G:** What's the use if he won't help us.

**G:** He shouldn't!

(The group becomes embroiled in whether or not they should go on a silence strike to punish the leader.)

**L:** Now look, you've shared a big hunk of experience together. Any time you're a mind to you can reach out and touch your symbols. What do they feel like?

**G:** Maybe we don't want to be members of a mass; just female blobs. Maybe we want to be us; individuals; ourselves.

**G:** A person can be himself and still be a part of something else. It's like being one with God.

(The group seems a trifle shocked into sobriety by this sincere reference to the Deity and then listens to Ba.'s private theory of "relative predestination," which it turns into a debate over free will.)

**G:** No, that isn't it. It isn't that I believe everything in my life is predetermined by God's will. It's relative. I am responsible for myself and I make decisions and they determine things and I take the consequences. But there are many things that affect me in my life that I am not responsible for—like my parents. And these things I believe are predetermined by God's will. I don't think it makes me a blob to have the comfort of leaning on God beyond what I can do for myself.
(Silence)

**G:** This is the first time I've ever come right out and said what I believe. I've started to a few times and people began to laugh so I kept it to myself. I was afraid it would sound foolish even in the group. I'm still not sure.

(The group supports her.)

**G:** No, it doesn't sound foolish at all!

(Discussion of the tendency to hold back, or apologize for, deep beliefs for fear they will be laughed at or ridiculed)

**G:** So where does free will come in?
**G:** I see it like this: I won't know what I'm coping with until after I've coped with it. Then I can look back and I've got free will over it. But meanwhile I can trust God's will.
**L:** Is that what you have been looking for, free will?
**G:** Could be.
**G:** We don't have free will here.
**G:** We couldn't handle it if we had it.
**G:** There's nothing stopping us.
**G:** I know, but we're putting our own restrictions on it, so we don't have it.
**G:** But that *is* free will if they're *our own* restrictions.
**G:** I'm not so sure they're our own.
**G:** We're free to the extent that we *want* to be.
**G:** Then we must not want to be.

**G:** So you go through school and what you should want the most you don't even want to discuss it. You want to resist it!

With the coming of spring the interests of research gave way to the opportunity of combining the group meetings with sunshine and grass. There were four unrecorded meetings following the twenty-fourth meeting in which the leader's primary aim was to facilitate the active facing of the approaching separation of the group as a group. It would perhaps be gratifying—insofar as departures from reality can be—to find the group forging still further ahead after its brief encounter with "genitality." It must be remembered, however, that the society of which these girls are members is not at all prepared to make a contract with them at such a level; and even if it were, as we know so well, genitality is not so easily gained a prize. It is closer to typically paradoxical psychoanalytic fact that frequent regression from genitality is at the same time the price and the reward of its achievement. Thus in the next meeting we find:

**G:** Let's sit in a square out here.

**G:** Let's all lie down and have a sun-bathing party.

**G:** Let's get some ice cream.

**L:** Anything goes—*as long* as you put it in words.

**G:** Oh, to hell with the agreement.

**G:** You (leader) *made* us agree. We had no choice.

**G:** If we can't get ice cream we'll go on a silence strike.

(Etc.)

In a very distinct sense then we may look upon these twenty-four group meetings as representing a slow and struggling, very much telescoped recapitulation of the female's emotional development insofar as we understand this development. We saw this struggled with in terms of the issues of trust, of autonomy, of initiative, of industry, and of identity. We saw these to be never far from their associated sexual and aggressive connotations in the unconscious, and therefore never far from inevitable frustration and the related need to find a safe outlet for the engendered hostility. And, finally, this evidence of partial re-integration in the group's brief flirtation with the issue of free will—not in the parroting intellectualisms of this familiar school issue, but emerging naturally and searchingly from the conflictful experiences of a group of students who had agreed to seek a relationship of verbal intimacy.

It will be noted that in this long account there have been very few striking expressions of consciousness of increased self-knowledge. At no point does the group suddenly stop and say: "Ah-hah! Now we are more aware of ourselves than before." For such assurance we are dependent on the phenomenological reports of the students at the conclusion of the course, and on the quantitative test findings. This, I believe, is as it should be. There are few resting places in a group's pursuit of self-awareness, except perhaps in the private reflections of its members. There is too little time, and, if new emotional vistas are indeed opening up, too much exploring to be done. And if greater emotional economies are being achieved it is to be hoped that the savings will be invested not in public testimonials but in an enriched carrying on of day to day living. Moreover, if the workshop is succeeding in encouraging and constructively guiding a preconscious re-living of previous emotional development, then we must look for the gains just there: *in the preconscious*, where, as we know, change is to be observed not *in* but *between* the lines. From this point of view there was the first meeting, which said: Why can we not remain passive and unresponsible, or be effortlessly transformed? And there was the twenty-fourth meeting, which said: So this is what we do, resist what we most desire—free will!

What may be inferred from between these lines is not that more of something has been *put in* the students, in which case we could point directly to the putting-in techniques. What is to be inferred, I think, is that education as ideally defined (c.f. Ch. 3) may have been approached.

As the *group* meetings were designed to serve the process of *assimilation*—to briefly call on the too overlooked psychology of Jean Piaget (76)—the *class* meetings were designed to serve the alternate stroke of effective adaptation, the process of *accommodation;* the terms being roughly suggestive of the therapeutic concepts "working through," and "insight attainment," respectively, and ultimately more appropriate, it seems to me, to the description of educational events.

The class meetings were run in a seminar fashion within a standard classroom setting complete with note-taking, hand-raising, etc. The subject was "psychology." No formal commitment was felt on the part of the instructor to any particular sub-division of psychology, nor to any particular scope of coverage. In short, the class meetings were a time when the spotlight on the self could be turned off, emotions could be left to shift for themselves, and everyone including the instructor could, in keeping with time-worn educational tradition, enjoy the feeling of random knowledge sifting down through crevices in the defenses.

The group leader became the class instructor, wielding authority in a manner consistent with the earlier emotional level at which the class meetings were pitched—complete with occasional verbal knuckle-rapping. After each group meeting the instructor would improvise two short fifteen or twenty minute lectures, taking his cues from the content of the group meeting (e.g., questions that he had openly referred to class meetings, and questioning remarks that had become lost in the tangentiality of the group's associations). He would begin the two subsequent class meetings with these lectures and then direct a class discussion relating to them. In this way the students were offered a smattering of many psychologies: experimental, comparative, social, dynamic, child, abnormal, and physiological.

It will be objected that this represents a singularly slip-shod approach to the subject matter of the course—an objection to which I subscribe. This is simply to admit that the subject matter was ill-chosen for the purposes of the experiment. If truth be known, it was not chosen at all, but dictated; firstly by the fact that it was the only subject for which I was equipped to hire on as a teacher, and secondly by the fact that it was the only subject in the established curriculum which was sufficiently expendable to rationalize away the administration's qualms over the methods to be employed. (The universities were not accepting the course for credit under any circumstances.) To be sure, the acid test of the method will come with its application to English or Mathematics—or better still to reading and writing. When we have advanced this far, however, I believe we shall see in clearer relief at least the same principles as emerged in the present obscured context.

The class meetings often lapsed into mildly cathartic sessions in which personally charged material (dreams, daydreams, childhood memories, family problems) were exchanged within the atmosphere of reduced personal responsibility engendered by the more authoritarian structure of the classroom. Student interactions which had the effect of producing tension such as direct confrontations, personal challenges, or expressions of hostility were referred by the instructor to the next group meeting. Thus out of the very bi-polarity of the workshop's structure an interesting form of resistance gave rise to a productive set of therapeutic and didactic techniques. The author came to refer in his thinking to the *reciprocity of the resistance*: The students very quickly came to recognize the respective defensive possibilities of the two situations. The group meetings, standing as they did for personal freedom of expression, came automatically to stand also for taking personal responsibility for what was expressed (i.e., for assuming a defenseless or self-acceptant position toward what was expressed). The class meetings, standing as they did for youthful dependence on authority, came automatically to stand for the shifting of responsibility onto the authority figure (i.e., for self-belittlement).

The group meeting was, of course, the situation where well tested defenses of the past were less applicable, and where new forms of defense had to be improvised—thus giving the group meetings their growth-conducive potential, regression being forced upon the adaptive powers of the members by way of expecting advanced progression. Recall the recurrent pressure to turn the group meetings into class meetings by introducing subject-rather than self-oriented discussions. As was clear in the accounts of the group meetings, the leader's technique in meeting this form of resistance was to consistently refer such discussions to the class meetings. This served a three-fold purpose. (1) It kept the self-relevant nature of the group meetings clearly in focus. (2) It offered the transference figure of the leader to the members as a focus for its hostility, thus allowing the hostility to be discharged in expressive rather than in repressive ways, in the process freeing the ego to use the resultant energy surplus in its re-integrative activities. (3) It brought the very forces of the resistance into play as *motivation* in support of the academic learning process, when the subject-matter, as subject-matter, was discussed very soon afterward in the appropriate context of the class meeting.*

There was a second way in which the class meeting came to be used in the service of resistance, which necessitated the reverse of this technique. It sometimes happened in the midst of the usually relaxed cathartic interplay that crept into the class discussions that individuals in the group would be tempted to reveal themselves in a subtle spirit of provocative irresponsibility. In this way they were taking advantage of the leader's implicit assumption of authoritative responsibility to ventilate that which they would find too threatening to accept personal responsibility for if the same material were to be expressed in a group meeting. When this was successful it had the repressive effect of a symptom; i.e., discharge without insight, the emotional undertone seeming to be: "He said it, not me" or "I said it, but he made me." It became important, therefore, for the leader to develop a sensitivity to this threshold of responsibility, and, when it was approached, to refer such discussions to the *group* meetings.

Thus, insofar as the resistance was reciprocally played off, as it were, the processes of accommodation and assimilation were guided toward a state of optimal equilibrium. In illustration of this technique let us reconsider the following interchange:

**G:** I thought of losing things in connection with forgetting our assignment.

**L:** What is it we're not sure of here that we always have been sure of?

**G:** Ourselves.

**G:** A teacher.

**G:** It's odd to have a teacher that just sits there. A teacher is usually entirely present or entirely absent.

**G:** What do you (leader) want?

**G:** Will you tell us why people forget things?

**L:** Yes, in the next *class* meeting.

**G:** Why not now?

**L:** That is not what we agreed to do together in the group meetings.

---

* This is a feature of the method to be most carefully observed when the method comes to be applied to more routine classroom subjects.

**G:** But you're the one who *knows* everything.

**G:** He doesn't know *everything*.

**G:** What are we supposed to discuss in this period?

In the following class meeting the leader-instructor presented a short lecture on "Why People Forget Things." The following major points were made:

1. People do not forget things in the sense that mental records of experiences are ever *lost*.
2. What we call forgetting refers to the human capacity of shifting an experience from one part of the mind to another, the latter being like a series of storage vaults some of whose doors are more easily opened than others.
3. The reasons for this capacity are reasons of expediency. The full meaning of any remembrance in the mind is in many of its "forgotten" roots and it is more convenient to remember just the remembrance than it is to keep everything constantly in mind; as it is more convenient to carry around dollar bills and let the gold lie buried than to carry around the gold.
4. There are different categories of "things forgotten."
   (1) The painful steps of things once learned with difficulty and now automatic, e.g., walking, talking, etc.
   (2) The mental images that we have no need for at the moment but can recall easily.
   (3) The mental images that we cannot recall at all but never feel any need to recall because we feel comfortable with their conscious representations (like money that we can trust).
   (4) The mental images which for reasons of painful associations are kept in a specially locked vault and which are troublesome because we cannot feel comfortable with their conscious representatives.
5. When we are asleep and not in need of conscious know-how we often take a private inventory of the storage vaults. These are called dreams.

At the conclusion of the lecture the class immediately asked if they could discuss their dreams, and this developed into a rather enjoyable and mutually supportive you-tell-me-your-dream-and-I'll-tell-you-mine kind of catharsis. Then the topic shifted to daydreams and then to imagination and the possible personal relevance of creative English compositions. At this point all eyes turned un-accountably toward one member (who it later developed was es-pecially known for her preoccupation with Poe and stories of sin-ister violence). It was at this point that the instructor, becoming vaguely aware of an increased atmosphere of classroom irresponsi-bility, suggested that the class was straying from the topic, with the reminder that this was the privilege only of the group meetings, and re-focused the discussion onto "Why People Forget Things."

There was one important role played by the class meetings that was not consciously planned, but which proved to be a vital part of the plan. The class meetings, as it turned out, served to meet the instructor's less mature needs fully as much as it served to meet those of the students. It is obvious that the group leader's personal involvement in the group's recapitulatory experience is necessarily an intense one. Just as necessary, however, is his need to restrain his expression of the personal aspect of that involvement. It is not always easy to remain passive in such a situation, i.e., not to "give the answer," and the more skillful the resistance becomes the stronger is the leader's temptation to be seduced out of his trans-ference role. Consequently, the intervening opportunities afforded by the class meetings for the leader to indulge the appropriate nar-cissistic need of the teacher, namely to teach what he is master of, was both welcome and constructive.

In conclusion, viewing the workshop as a whole, on a continuum from purely clinical, personality-centered therapy to purely aca-demic, subject-centered coursework, it would appear to fall some distance left of center. As a workshop method within the broader framework of social psychology the self-knowledge workshop is the diametric opposite of Levinson's Intergroup Relations Work-shop (60). Where the latter sought directly to reduce ethnic preju-dice in such a way as indirectly to affect constructive personality changes, the former sought directly to affect constructive person-ality changes in such a way as indirectly to reduce ethnic prejudice.

## CHAPTER FIVE

# EVALUATION

At THE CONCLUSION of the workshop the members were asked to make a one or two page statement in response to the question: "What effects do you feel your workshop experiences have had on you?" Such documents are notoriously difficult to evaluate, especially when they are requested of students by teachers. There is always the knotty problem of deciding if what is said is really meant, or if it represents the student's estimation of what he is *expected* to say. In making this decision one is often most influenced by the subtle stylistic aspects of the statement and what one reads between the lines. Very often what is inferred in this manner is the opposite of what is said. For example, there is the girl who writes: "Mr. Jones, you gave me a pain at times when you wouldn't answer our questions directly," and then ends her statement: "Best of luck to you." One is inclined to take pretty much at face value whatever *else* she has said, because she has demonstrated that she felt no great need to keep her strong feelings, negative or positive, to herself. There is, on the other hand, the Southern belle who writes: "Gosh, if only I could put into words how sincerely this has been a God sent blessing to me, I certainly in every way would." It is difficult to shake the premonition in this case that the young lady protests overly much, and one is therefore inclined to reserve judgement on the issue of how much of a "blessing" the experience has *really* been to her. If she cannot find words for her positive feelings one wonders what else she has not found words for.

One of the girls who, in my opinion, did not benefit optimally from her workshop experience had this to say:

> I think that I have learned a great deal from the psychology class periods, but I feel that I have not gained anything from the discussion periods on Wednesday morning. I have been very disappointed with the group meetings and I have been disgusted for the past eight weeks and feel that we have accomplished nothing. To be frank, I think it is your fault and not the class.

We conclude that to a considerable extent the workshop failed to achieve its aim for this girl and we are inclined to accept her own account of this failure at face value in view of her obvious freedom in expressing it. We are, of course, inclined to take some solace in the observation that this very freedom of expression was, indeed, one of the aims of the workshop, even though we hold to the wish that her conscious retrospective of it could have been a more pleasant one for her.

One of the girls who, in the author's opinion, benefited most from her workshop experience had this to say:

> To tell you the truth, I am not sure. I enjoyed this class, and and believe that I have gotten quite a bit from it, but just what this is I am not sure. I do know that I am a different person in the group meetings. In the class meetings I am like I am in every other class, but in the discussion group I am someone else. I don't know if I am my real self or if it is just that I act different.
>
> I do know I can feel a change inside me but I can't explain it. It's a sort of feeling of reassurance that I can be a person like anyone else, that I can belong, but most of all that I can belong when and how I want to. I have discovered that I can change my mind about things I have once formed in my mind whenever I want. I have learned that I can like people if I want to (I used to hate people as a whole). I have learned to wonder or question things or ideas instead of accepting what I see or hear. But with all the new feelings that are good I have built up fears. I have learned that life is big and wonderful but I am now afraid of its bigness and just how wonderful it really is. I'm afraid to say or do certain things for fear of what my mind will do or say about this. I'm afraid to face the big truth—life. All of this I used never to question. I'd accept it and that was all but now I've learned some new dimensions, "why" being the biggest, next "how" and "when." I never saw these before.

To sum all this up, I have changed. Whether I like it or not, I can't say. I am different, and it will take a while to get used to being someone else. I think you saw a lot of this since the "great mixup" at the beginning of the year. I will give you credit on this point, I am one person that the self-knowledge workshop worked on. I did learn more about myself. Hope you have as much luck next year and the years that follow. Good luck!

We conclude that the workshop has achieved its aim to the maximum degree possible for this girl; and we conclude this not only on the basis of what she says but even more on the basis of the intense personal involvement that is reflected in her manner of saying it; of her inclination to qualify and to temper her positive statements, to balance them with like tempered negative statements, to reserve judgment in realistic ways, and to phrase her statements in the language of clearly unfettered introspection.

In contrast to these, the girl who, in the author's opinion, benefited least from her workshop experience had this to say:

The main effect that the workshop experience had on me is a deeper understanding of myself. I actually feel that I have achieved the goal of the workshop, "self-knowledge." Through this deeper understanding of myself I have learned to better understand others. During the course of the year I also feel that I have gained a great deal of confidence in myself—a building up of the ego.

In the informal discussions I found it very interesting to try and figure out the emotions and thoughts behind each girl in the class. I also enjoyed comparing my ideas or opinions to the ideas or opinions of the rest of the class.

Mr. Jones, I have one criticism. Had you led the class more I think that the discussion periods would have proved more worthwhile. Probably if you had entered more into our conversation and enlightened us to a greater extent there would have been fewer silent periods. Other than that one criticism I feel that my time was well spent by taking psychology this year.

We conclude that despite her "one criticism" this girl had hardly been reached by the workshop. There is nothing in her choice of words to suggest that what she says is anything more than a reflection of what she feels she "ought" to say. She feels called upon to apologize for giving expression to the one aspect of the resistance that had long since become a cliché in the group meetings, and even if we were not inclined to question her grossly unqualified opening testimonial to having "achieved the goal of the workshop—self-knowledge," we are driven to discredit it when in her closing sentence she refers to having taken "psychology this year."

With these illustrations of the author's bias in evaluating such statements the following attempt at quantitative summarization:

The following criteria were considered to reflect the *presence* of increased self-acceptance:

1. More reference to personal change ("more confidence," "get along with people better," etc.) than to academic achievement ("learned a lot," "enjoyed taking psychology," etc.).

2. Inclusion of *both* positive and negative opinions of the workshop experience and/or the instructor.

3. More evidence of personal introspection (signs of specificity, frankness, individualized expressions, etc.) than of clichéd conformity ("greatly enriched by the opportunity . . . ," "helped me mature," etc.).

The following criteria were considered to reflect the absence of increased self-acceptance:

1. More reference to academic achievement than to personal change (see above).

2. Grossly one-sided positive or negative appraisals of the workshop and/or the instructor. As suggested above, the one-sided negative appraisal is considered indicative of some movement in the direction of self-acceptance but because it is considered to be minimal it is included among the "absence" criteria.

3. More evidence of clichéd conformity than of personal introspection.

The ratings of the phenomenological reports of both workshop groups are summarized in terms of degrees of "success" in Table 2.

TABLE 2

SUMMARY OF RATINGS OF EVALUATION PROTOCOLS

| Evaluation Category | No. of Protocols |
|---|---|
| Optimally successful (+++) | 9* |
| Marginally successful (++−) | 7 |
| Marginally unsuccessful (−−+) | 1 |
| Unsuccesful (−−−) | 2 |

* To be included in the "optimally successful" category a protocol had to meet all three criteria for the presence of increased self-acceptance. Protocols in the "marginally successful" category met two such "presence" criteria and one "absence" criterion; in the "marginally unsuccessful" category, two "absence" criteria and one "presence" criterion; and in the "unsuccessful" category, three "absence" criteria.

Table 3 indicates that no significant differences existed between any of the groups on any of the measures of self-acceptance at the time of initial testing. To the extent that the aims of the workshop were fulfilled we expect a significant shift in the direction of increased self-acceptance in the experimental group mean on each measure. In more formal terms we predict that the experimental group will show a significant change in the designated direction on all the measures, and that the control groups will show no significant change. Lord's one-sample t-Test (71) was employed to test the validity of these predictions. The pertinent data are presented in Table 4.

TABLE 3

INITIAL STANDING OF THE EXPERIMENTAL AND CONTROL GROUPS ON THE VARIOUS MEASURES OF SELF-ACCEPTANCE*

|  | Experimental Group | Matched Control Group | Alternate School Control Group |
|---|---|---|---|
| No. of Cases | 19 | 19 | 19 |
| Berger SA Score |  |  |  |
| Mean | 132.39 | 140.58 | 134.61 |
| Range | 73 | 60 | 61 |
| NS Score |  |  |  |
| Mean | 18.37 | 18.47 | 18.00 |
| Range | 26 | 25 | 24 |
| ET-A Score |  |  |  |
| Mean | 34.59 | 33.82 | 39.78 |
| Range | 75 | 71 | 77 |
| NS-3 Score |  |  |  |
| Mean | 11.95 | 12.00 | 12.00 |
| Range | 17 | 15 | 16 |

NS-1 Score

| | | | |
|---|---|---|---|
| Mean | 6.53 | 6.63 | 6.00 |
| Range | 12 | 11 | 15 |

* On no measure do any of the research groups differ significantly from one another in their initial mean scores.

TABLE 4

CHANGE IN AVERAGE SCORE ON THE VARIOUS SELF-ACCEPTANCE MEASURES FROM INITIAL TO FINAL TESTING

| | Experimental Group | Matched Control Group | Alternate School Control Group |
|---|---|---|---|
| No. of Cases | 19 | 19 | 19 |
| Bogardus Social Distance Scale (increase predicted) | | | |
| Change score ($M_2-M_1$) | +5.33 | −5.11 | −1.61 |
| "t" | 1.81* | 1.44 | .58 |
| NS Score (decrease predicted) | | | |
| Change score ($M_2-M_1$) | −2.32 | +1.64 | −3.37 |
| "t" | 2.32* | 1.54 | 2.34* |
| ET-A Score (increase predicted) | | | |
| Change score ($M_2-M_1$) | +15.17 | −6.81 | −5.67 |
| "t" | 5.65** | 1.39 | .99 |
| NS-3 Score (decrease predicted) | | | |
| Change score ($M_2-M_1$) | −2.11 | 0 | +.89 |
| "t" | 3.07** | 0 | 1.01 |
| NS-1 Score (decrease predicted) | | | |
| Change score ($M_2-M_1$) | −.37 | +1.42 | +2.47 |
| "t" | .48 | 1.50 | 2.19* |

In the table "$M_2$" is the final mean, "$M_1$" the initial mean; since change is computed as $M_2-M_1$, positive values indicate an increase, negative values a decrease.

An experimental group "t" value followed by a single asterisk is significant at the 5 per cent level of confidence; a double asterisk indicates the 1 per cent level or better. For a sample of 19 cases, using a one-tailed test of significance (since the workshop predictions had directionality), a "t" of at least 1.73 is needed for the 5 per cent level, and 2.55 for the 1 per cent level.

A control group "t" value followed by an asterisk is significant at the 5 per cent level. For a sample of 19 cases, using a two-tailed test of significance (since the control group predictions lacked directionality) a "t" of at least 2.10 is needed for the 5 per cent level.

Both the qualitative and the quantitative sets of data strongly support the conclusion that the workshop *did* achieve its aim of facilitating increased self-acceptance in its members. The ratings of the members' evaluation statements indicate that for sixteen of the nineteen members the workshop was at least marginally successful. The quantitative findings are equally forceful in their implications. The general pattern of the results can be stated simply: The experimental group has undergone a significant change in the predicted direction on all measures. The control groups, on the other hand, show a consistent shift in the direction of *decreased* self-acceptance on all measures. These decreases although unpredicted are significant.

The Berger scale findings indicate that the experimental group has undergone a significant increase in conscious, expressed attitudes of self-acceptance. The sentence completion test findings indicate not only that the experimental group tends significantly less often at the conclusion of the workshop to deny self reference to its sentence completion responses in general, but significantly *more* often to accept those responses that are judged to be "ego threatening" in nature. The implication is that the changes in the experimental group's *conscious* reorganization of its conflict material has been accompanied by similar changes at deeper levels of personality organization. Since within a given protocol the sum of the NS-3 (projectivity) and the NS-1 (anti-intraception) scores is equal to the NS (self-rejection) score, it would appear that practically the entire increase in the experimental group's attitudes of self-acceptance may be attributed to a *decrease* in its tendency to handle ego-alien content via externalizing or projective defences. Anti-intraceptive organizational mechanisms, on the other hand, have remained relatively stable.

The consistency and magnitude of the indications of decreasing attitudes of self-acceptance in the control groups during the experimental period serve to place the experimental data in even more meaningful perspective. In view of the small samples involved, I shall avoid drawing any sweeping inferences to the nature of adolescent personality development. It is tempting to relate the control group findings to an assumption discussed above, concerning the neurotogenic nature of existing educational practices, but here too I shall defer to the limitations of the sample.

It *is* within reasonable scope of the data, however, to conclude that within the context in which it functioned the workshop had the effect of counteracting existing forces in the life setting of the members that were significantly conducive to self *rejection* and, *in addition*, of facilitating forces that were significantly conducive to self *acceptance*.

When we break the self rejection (NS) scores for the control groups down into their projective and anti-intraceptive elements, we note an interesting dovetailing of the control data with the experimental data: Whereas the *increase* in self acceptance attributed to the experimental group seems largely to be accounted for by a *decrease* in projectivity, while anti-intraception remains relatively stable, the reverse is the case with the control groups. Here the *decrease* in self acceptance seems largely to be accounted for by an *increase* in anti-intraception, while projectivity remains relatively stable. We shall return to these findings when we consider the results on the ethnic attitude scales.

In summary, we recall this telling protest from one of the group members after a particularly difficult step in the direction of accepting personal responsibility for previously disowned feelings:

> "I feel completely uninhibited now, and in a few minutes the bell is going to ring and I have to go to a class where it's 'Yes Ma'am—No Ma'am' and put yourself on report if you breathe the wrong way, and that's not good for me. Psychology is supposed to help you think better. When I leave here I can't think at all for two hours. Can you sit there and say that is good for me?"

It appears that it was.

# PART TWO
## Effects on Ethnic Prejudice

## CHAPTER SIX

# PERSPECTIVE

THE FOLLOWING statements convey an overview of the ethnic prejudice research activity that has reached a climax in recent years:

Bruner, in his 1950 review of social psychology (20) states:

Ethnocentrism and its determinants continue to be a major focus of research in social psychology. A brief review of the past year's work indicates that in this area perhaps more than in any other part of attitude research, the resources of many other parts of psychology as well as other social sciences have been brought to bear.

Crutchfield, in his 1954 review of social psychology (25) states:

A steady stream of studies of enthnic prejudice continues to flow, focused primarily on the determinants and correlates of prejudice, the effect of personal contact on prejudice, the relation of expression of prejudice to overt behavior, and the comparison of prejudice among various groups. To this reviewer there seem to be few truly outstanding developments in the field during the year's work. The studies are mainly extensions of lines of inquiry previously set in motion, rather than significant departures or innovations in theory and method.

An independent review of the literature points up a deficiency in the extension of those lines of inquiry to which Crutchfield refers: Two broad categories of psychological factors predisposing to prejudice have been described and investigated; sociocultural and psychodynamic factors (3). The complementary approach of systematically evaluating programs for the *reduction* of prejudice, based on the findings of these investigations, has been largely concerned with sociocultural factors (9, 48, 78, 83). Of the seven approaches to the reduction of prejudice reviewed by Allport (3), which might be said to deal in some way with *psychodynamic* factors, only one—individual therapy, which can hardly qualify as a "program"—can avoid the criticism of being naively symptom-oriented, if we allow the term "psychodynamic" its usual connotations. It is this line of inquiry that Part Two pursues.

The psychodynamic or "indirect" approach to the reduction of race prejudice by way of educational or therapeutic programs directed toward underlying emotional factors is not unique, although it is rare compared to the number of studies relating the *development* of prejudice to personal-emotional factors.

Wieder (99) conducted a controlled study of this type in which an experimental group of college students differed from the control group in having been enrolled for a semester in a course entitled "Practical Psychology." The technique employed was an interesting modification of the psychodramatic and sociodramatic methods developed by Moreno and Jennings. The E and F scales were used as measures of prejudice; the Minnesota Multiphasic Personality Inventory and the Bills Index of Adjustment and Values were the personality measures. Wieder reports a significant decrease in the E and F means of the experimental group and significant changes in the predicted direction on two of the four Bills scales. Other findings were negative.

Asch (11) conducted a similarly controlled study in which an experimental group of college students differed from its control group in having been enrolled for a semester in a "non-directive, student-centered" psychology course. Increased self-knowledge was the unstated aim of the course. Qualitative evidence and before and after MMPI profiles indicated significantly increased relative "adjustment" in the experimental group. A decreased mean score on the Bogardus Social Distance scale was reported for both experimental and control groups; neither was significant.

Haimowitz (47) reports an uncontrolled study in which the Bogardus Scale was administered to twenty-four Veterans Administration personnel (aged 25 to 60) before and after a six weeks training experience as members of "Rogerian" therapeutic groups.

The findings indicated a significant change in the direction of "more friendly attitudes."

These studies have in common with each other and with the present one the basic idea of "indirect" reduction of prejudice. They are not consistent with one another nor with the present study in their results, in the means they employed to affect the results, nor in the populations in whom the results were observed. We see no purpose, therefore, in forcing a detailed comparison where the details are not comparable.

The general weight of evidence produced by the preceding studies vaguely suggests that "indirect" approaches (variously defined) *do* have the effect of reducing prejudice. In view of the amount of time that goes into planning and carrying through such programs it is regrettable that the evaluation methods were as limited as they were. The systematic crux of the "indirect" design is not that this or that personality centered experience can be demonstrated to reduce prejudice (although this is not uninteresting in itself). The salient point to be shown is that *demonstrated* changes in *theoretically related* personality factors (however produced) have this effect.

The present research was planned so that changes in personality variables theoretically related to prejudice could first be evaluated, and the prediction of prejudice reduction based on these findings, not on the educational method itself.

*CHAPTER SEVEN*

# THEORY

$T$HE HYPOTHESES which the study was designed to test derive from the psychodynamic theory of ethnic prejudice—as distinct, for example, from the "sociocultural," "phenomenological" or other convergent theories of prejudice enumerated in Allport's multi-deterministic approach to the subject (3). The psychodynamic theory of prejudice is rooted primarily in psychoanalytic personality theory. In its relationship to psychoanalytic theory, moreover, unlike another category of psychoanalytically derived theories, it enjoys a position within general psychological theory that has become largely free from controversy and theoretical hair splitting. Its central proposition may as readily be generated by "neo-Freudian" interpersonal relations theory, or by "Rogerian" self-concept theory, as by "orthodox Freudian" theory.

This proposition states: The emotional rejection of any attribute *external* to the self is an indirect expression of the emotional rejection of some attribute *internal* to the self. The following statements, which denote the same proposition, serve to lend it connotational enrichment while also demonstrating the scope of accord that accrues to it.

Sullivan (95) states:

"... as one respects oneself so one can respect others ... If there is a valid and real attitude toward the self that attitude will manifest as valid and real towards others. It is not that as ye judge so shall ye be judged, but as you judge yourself so shall you judge others."

94

Erikson, (31) in reference to adolescent development, which is particularly apt in view of our sample, states:

"It is difficult to be tolerant if deep down you are not quite sure you are a man (or a woman), that you will ever grow together again and be attractive, that you will be able to master your drives, that you really know who you are, that you know what you want to be . . ."

Dorsey (28) puts it somewhat more colorfully:

"The individual who is very much of a riot within himself needs outside riots in order to exercise and justify his makeup."

In its more intimate derivation from general psychoanalytic personality theory the psychodynamic theory of prejudice provides a schema that includes both genetic and dynamic points of reference. It asserts that the child whose emotional growth is crucially influenced by rigid parental discipline, conditional affection, and intra-family relationships based upon sharply fixed roles of dominance and submission, develops a readiness for the acquisition of prejudiced ethnic attitudes. This readiness is said to be engineered by a familiar pattern of psychodynamics in which the hostility toward the parents that has been generated by these conditions is repressed along with other emotional strivings not supported by the parents—leaving the child free to admit to consciousness only the positive side of his ambivalences. The unacceptable strivings are then projected, and the hostility displaced, onto out-groups.

Accordingly, in the summaries of evidence advanced in support of the theory we find the "tolerant personality" described as having evolved systems of defense based upon "self-awareness" and "internalization" of anxiety-provoking stimuli; social values based upon "self-realized" experience; family values emanating from a basic "love orientation"; and a type of cognitive functioning that is "flexible." On the other hand the "prejudiced" or "authoritarian" personality is described as having evolved systems of defense based upon "repression" and "externalization"; social values that are "conventional"; family values emanating from a basic "power-orientation"; and a type of cognitive functioning that is "rigid."

This account is representative of the bi-polar syndrome approach that seems to characterize psychodynamic studies of prejudice. It has been applied to many and various levels of attention to personality-centered prejudice. It is not beyond criticism especially as it resembles the persistent, albeit spurious, explanation of health via denoting absence of illness. However, the evidence in support of the bi-polar syndromes is impressive (1, 2, 3, 10, 17, 20, 25, 32, 35, 37, 58, 63, 67, 81), and common to all of them are references to the same fundamental principle. Frenkel-Brunswick, in summarizing a large portion of the definitive work on the "authoritarian personality" (2) makes a convincing statement of this principle:

> "Regardless of whether the specific topic was that of ambivalence, or aggression, or passivity, or some other related feature of personality dynamics, *the outstanding finding* was that the extremely unprejudiced individual tends to manifest a greater readiness to become aware of unacceptable tendencies and impulses in himself. The prejudiced individual, on the other hand, is more apt *not* to face these tendencies openly and thus to fail in integrating them satisfactorily with the conscious image he has of himself."

The weight of evidence issuing from the wave of prejudice research that followed World War II is testimony to the sturdiness of this theory. The evidence, however, is almost entirely *correlational* in nature. It has accumulated, that is to say, from studies that have sought to determine the personality features of individuals who are demonstrably "high" in prejudice, and of individuals who are demonstrably "low" in prejudice. There have been conspicuously few studies that have sought to observe the effects upon prejudiced attitudes of experimentally induced *changes* in these personality features. The functional social value of the many studies now on record relating ethnic prejudice to psychodynamic factors must therefore be considered incomplete and the theoretical implications of these studies not fully explored until it is demonstrated that appropriate personality *changes* lead to the reduction of prejudiced attitudes.

The study under discussion, then, was designed to be an experimental cross-check on the correlational evidence already on hand in support of the theory. Hence the question that generated the research design: Can already acquired prejudiced attitudes be reduced by appropriately varying the more generic personality components that are theoretically assumed to predispose people toward the acquisition of prejudiced attitudes, without attempting directly to change the attitudes themselves? Or, more to the moment: Does the increase in attitudes of self-tolerance, demonstrated to have been facilitated by the workshop, result in a *simultaneous* decrease in attitudes of ethnic intolerance?

## CHAPTER EIGHT

# RESULTS AND CONCLUSIONS

IN ORDER to document the "indirectness" called for by the research design the students were asked at the conclusion of the workshop, after the final testing, to state in writing: "To what extent do you feel that the topic of race prejudice has been dealt with in this course, either in the class or in the group meetings?" The answers are included in the appendix. They indicate that the demands of the research design have been met, i.e., that the topic of race prejudice was not directly dealt with in the workshop.

In comparing the initial and final scores on the social attitude measures the same hypothetical and statistical procedures were followed as were applied to the data on self-acceptance. Table 5 indicates that no significant differences existed between the experimental and matched control groups on any of the social attitude measures at the time of initial testing. It indicates also, however, that the alternate school control group *did* differ significantly at various points with both the experimental and the matched control groups. These differences occur on the Bogardus, the E, and the F scales, and indicate that the alternate school control group entered the experimental interval showing significantly less evidence of race prejudice and "authoritarianism" than did the other two groups; considerably less, moreover, than does the general population, according to demographic reports on these scales. The control value of the matched group is thus enhanced since we are required to entertain the possibility of a statistical regression effect as at least partially contributing to the observed changes in the alternate school control group on these variables.

To the extent that increased attitudes of self tolerance result in a simultaneous decrease in attitudes of ethnic intolerance we expect

TABLE 5

INITIAL STANDING OF THE EXPERIMENTAL AND CONTROL GROUPS ON THE VARIOUS
SOCIAL ATTITUDE MEASURES

|  | Experimental Group* | Matched Control Group* | Alternate School Control Group |
|---|---|---|---|
| No. of Cases | 19 | 19 | 19 |
| Bogardus Social Distance Scale | | | |
| Mean | 90.00 | 75.05 | 67.37** |
| Range | 105 | 100 | 93 |
| E Scale | | | |
| Mean | 43.842 | 43.000 | 29.421*** |
| Range | 52 | 57 | 35 |
| F Scale | | | |
| Mean | 51.053 | 53.316 | 44.368**** |
| Range | 44 | 26 | 37 |
| TFI Scale | | | |
| Mean | 49.421 | 45.211 | 43.526 |
| Range | 25 | 27 | 38 |

\* On no measure do the experimental and matched control groups differ significantly from one another.

\*\* In its initial mean score on the Bogardus scale the alternate school control group differs significantly (1 per cent level) from the experimental group.

\*\*\* In its initial mean score on the E scale the alternate school control group differs significantly (1 per cent level) from both the experimental and the matched control groups.

\*\*\*\* In its initial mean score on the F scale the alternate school control group differs significantly (5 per cent level) from the matched control group.

a significant downward shift in the experimental group mean on each of the social attitude measures. Accordingly we predict that the experimental group will show a significant change in the downward direction on all the measures, and that the control groups will show no significant change. The pertinent data are presented in Table 6.

At first glance it would appear that the data strongly support all of the predictions. On all four scales the experimental group shows a downward shift significant at better than the 1 per cent level of confidence. On no scale do either of the control groups show a significant change. However, closer inspection of the *pattern* of this data shows an interesting departure from the pattern of the data on self-acceptance. The changes in *self-acceptance* shown by both control groups were consistently in a direction *opposite* to the changes shown by the experimental group. The changes in *social* attitudes shown by the control groups, on the other hand, were consistently in the *same* direction* as those shown by the experimental group, although none reached significance.

A *one sample test* was sufficient to evaluate the *self-acceptance* data. Due to the pattern of directionality in that data if *absolute* change in the experimental group was found to be significant then *relative* change between the experimental and control groups would necessarily be at least as significant. In the *social attitude*

TABLE 6

CHANGE IN AVERAGE SCORE ON THE VARIOUS SOCIAL ATTITUDE
MEASURES FROM INITIAL TO FINAL TESTING

|  | Experimental Group | Matched Control Group | Alternate School Control Group |
|---|---|---|---|
| *No. of Cases* | 19 | 19 | 19 |
| Bogardus Social Distance Scale |  |  |  |
| Change score $(M_2-M_1)$ | − 18.21 | − 5.05 | − .79 |
| "t" | 3.55** | 1.25 | .16 |
| E Scale |  |  |  |
| Change score $(M_2-M_1)$ | − 5.895 | − 4.947 | +1.368 |
| "t" | 3.04** | 1.52 | .58 |
| F Scale |  |  |  |
| Change score $(M_2-M_1)$ | − 6.685 | − 4.684 | − 1.421 |
| "t" | 2.90** | 1.97 | .56 |
| TFI Scale |  |  |  |
| Change score $(M_2-M_1)$ | − 7.947 | − .158 | − 2.842 |
| "t" | 3.26** | .08 | 1.18 |

In the table, "$M_2$" is the final mean, "$M_1$" the initial mean; since change is computed as $M_2-M_1$, positive values indicate an increase, negative values a decrease.

An experimental group "t" value followed by a single asterisk is significant at the 5 per cent level of confidence; a double asterisk indicates the 1 per cent level or better. For a sample of 19 cases, using a one-tailed test of significance (since the workshop predictions had directionality), a "t" of at least 1.73 is needed for the 5 per cent level, and 2.55 for the 1 per cent level.

A control group "t" value followed by an asterisk is significant at the 5 per cent level. For a sample of 19 cases, using a two-tailed test of significance (since the control group predictions lacked directionality) a "t" of at least 2.10 is needed for the 5 per cent level.

* The one exception to this pattern is the change score of the alternate school control group on the E scale. In view of the slight degree of this inconsistency and of the probability of its being partially due to statistical regression we are led to discount it.

data, however, the pattern of directionality raises the possibility of absolute change being significant and relative change not. We are to apply an additional *two sample* test of significance to these data, therefore, in order to reckon with the possibility that the findings are being applied to the predictions in a way that was made spurious by the form in which the predictions had been stated.

Consequently we now predict that the experimental group will have shown a significantly *greater* change in the downward direction on all social attitude measures, than did the control groups in the same direction. Furthermore we predict that there will have been no significant differences in either direction between the change scores of the Matched and Alternate School control groups. Lord's two-sample "t" test was employed to test the validity of these predictions. The pertinent data are presented in Table 7.

The data support the second of these predictions. The differences between the Matched and Alternate School control groups are not significant. Moreover, these differences are slight when compared to the differences between each control group and the experimental group.

The main prediction is still supported by the difference scores on the Bogardus and the TFI scales. We are led to discount the significance of the difference between the Experimental and Alternate School control groups on the E scale because of the probable influence of the regression effect previously noted. The data from the *E and F scales* contradict the initial findings in that they *do not* support the main prediction.

In interpreting these findings much depends upon whether reason follows, or is outdone, by ultra-conservatism in their statistical treatment. As regards those attitudes measured by the Bogardus and the TFI scales the evidence is strongly in support of the predictions by the most stringent test. As regards those attitudes measured by the E and F scales the predictions are upheld by the less conservative test only. It is notable that on no scale does the evidence run counter to prediction. A cautious interpretation of the totality of the findings would be that while the personality changes effected in the experimental group do result simultaneously in the predicted changes in ethnic attitudes on all of the measures, an un-

## TABLE 7

RELATIVE DIFFERENCES BETWEEN THE AVERAGE CHANGE SCORES OF
THE VARIOUS GROUPS ON THE SOCIAL ATTITUDE MEASURES

| | Experimental Group$_1$ — Matched Control Group$_2$ | Experimental Group$_1$ — Alternate School Control Group$_2$ | Matched Control Group — Alternate School Control Group |
|---|---|---|---|
| *No. of Cases* | 38 | 38 | 38 |
| Bogardus Social Distance Scale | | | |
| Difference Score | | | |
| $[(M_2-M_1)_1-(M_2-M_1)_2]$ | — 13.16 | — 17.42 | 4.26 |
| "t" | 2.03* | 2.46** | .07 |
| E Scale | | | |
| Difference Score | | | |
| $[(M_2-M_1)_1-(M_2-M_1)_2]$ | — .948 | — 7.263 | 3.579 |
| "t" | .26 | 2.41* | 1.58 |
| F Scale | | | |
| Difference Score | | | |
| $[(M_2-M_1)_1-(M_2-M_1)_2]$ | — 2.001 | — 5.264 | 3.263 |
| "t" | .61 | 1.57 | .95 |
| TFI Scale | | | |
| Difference Score | | | |
| $[(M_2-M_1)_1-(M_2-M_1)_2]$ | — 7.789 | — 5.105 | 2.684 |
| "t" | 2.52** | 1.52 | .87 |

In the table $(M_2-M_1)_1$ and $(M_2-M_1)_2$ are the change scores of the correspondingly denoted groups in the headings of the table. Since the difference scores are computed $[(M_2-M_1)_1-(M_2-M_1)_2]$, positive values indicate a relative increase, negative values a relative decrease.

A "t" value followed by a single asterisk is significant at the 5 per cent level of confidence; a double asterisk indicates the 1 per cent level of confidence or better. For a combined sample of 38 cases, using a one-tailed test of significance (since the workshop predictions had directionality) a "t" of at least 1.69 is needed for the 5 per cent level, and 2.44 for the 1 per cent level.

The matched vs. alternate school difference scores represent absolute rather than relative differences since the predictions pertinent to these scores lacked directionality. They are therefore not assigned positive or negative values and are accordingly set off from the table of relative differences. For a sample of 38 cases, using a two-tailed test of significance, a "t" of at least 2.01 is needed for the 5 per cent level.

controlled variable has effected non-significant, but appreciable, similar changes in the control subjects on two of the measures.

We conclude that the effects of the increase in attitudes of self-acceptance in the experimental group have been (1) a significant relative change in the predicted direction in the social attitudes measured by the TFI scale; (2) a non-significant relative change in the predicted direction in the social attitudes measured by the F scale; (3) a significant relative decrease in attitudes of ethnic prejudice as measured by the Bogardus scale; and (4) a non-significant relative decrease in attitudes of ethnic prejudice as measured by the E scale.

The TFI scale has a unique position in the research design. In the first place, it is not a measure of ethnic prejudice as such, although it is often included in batteried measurements of prejudice. Actually, while its high intercorrelation with the E scale shows that what it measures (liberal versus authoritarian family ideology) is very closely associated with the existence of prejudice, it is more to the point to say that it measures the *perpetuation* of prejudice than to say that it measures prejudice as such. In the second place, we are not justified to conclude that the change findings of the TFI scale have been effected by *indirect* means. Insofar as the workshop, as a school course, had a consciously focused subject, which the instructor endeavored to "teach," that subject *was* the family and its ideological issues. Moreover, while the author was careful to avoid the very subject of prejudice, much less to indulge his own views on it, he saw it as the appropriate task of the workshop in attempting to "liberalize" self attitudes, to deal actively, directly and solicitously with issues of family ideology. If we view the workshop as a school course, then, which indeed it was, we must interpret the TFI findings much as we might interpret a final examination. The course was successful in conveying the conscious subject matter which it sought to convey; not necessarily anything more.

We are prompted still further to entertain conservatism in interpreting the results when we consider the non-significant reduction of authoritarianism as measured by the F scale. Here again the F scale is not, strictly speaking, a measure of prejudice but it *is* a measure of that constellation of ideological values which we believe to sustain prejudice. With regard to "indirectness" we may view the workshop's influence on the F scale as having been less direct than is the case with the TFI but still more direct than with the E scale, which supposedly measures prejudice as such, and on which the magnitude of relative decrease is almost negligible.

If we consider only the results of the TFI, F, and E scales, therefore, we must conclude that the workshop has resulted in a significant relative decrease in those attitudes that *perpetuate* race prejudice; a non-significant relative increase in those attitudes that *sustain* race prejudice; and almost no relative decrease in prejudiced attitudes *as such*. Furthermore we must conclude that the effectiveness of the workshops is in linear relation to the directness of its aims. The general sense of both conclusions is contrary to prediction.

The value of the multi-dimensional approach to the measurement of social atitudes is underscored by the contrast between the results of the E scale and the results of the Bogardus scale. Both scales yield measures of race prejudice as such; and both sets of results can have been influenced by the workshop only by the most indirect means. However, where the relative decrease on the E scale is negligible the relative decrease on the Bogardus scale is significant.

If the reliability and validity of both scales* had not so often in the past been demonstrated we would be tempted to look for flaws in the measuring instruments. As it is we must assume that both results are valid, and accept this disparity as a stimulus to more detailed considerations. To this end, and taking a more perspicacious view of the two measuring instruments, we note two respectively distinguishing characteristics. The E scale accentuates the *ideological* aspects of prejudice, and it does this by asking a person to state the extent of his agreement with a series of prejudiced clichés ("Most Negroes would become overbearing and disagreeable if not kept in their place"). The Bogardus scale, on the other hand, accentuates the *action-prone* aspects of prejudice by asking a person to state the degree of social distance he would, indeed, tolerate with respect to a series of ethnic groups ("According to my first feeling reactions I would willingly admit 'Chinese,' 'Hindus,' 'Jews,' etc. to 'citizenship in my country,' 'to my street as neighbors,' 'to close kinship by marriage,' etc."). In other words the E scale asks

---

* It is remarkable how seldom the literature reports these two scales to have been applied together. Of the few studies reported where prejudice reduction has been sought via psychodynamic change, all have used one or the other; none have previously used both.

a person what he *thinks* about *in*tolerance; the Bogardus scale asks a person what he would *do* about tolerance. Normally we would expect these instruments to be interchangeable since, normally, we would expect tolerant actions to be in close inverse relation to intolerant ideas. The findings of this research, however, seem to prove the exception in this regard.

These considerations recall an elementary distinction made by Allport in defining the problem of race prejudice (3):

> ". . . an adequate definition of prejudice contains two essential ingredients. There must be an *attitude* of favor or disfavor; and it must be related to an over-generalized (and therefore erroneous) *belief*"

Allport concedes our previous assumption of E scale–Bogardus scale interchangeability when he states: "In modern researches it turns out that people who express a high degree of antagonistic *attitudes** on a test for prejudice, also show that they *believe** to a high degree that the groups they are prejudiced against have a large number of objectionable qualities." However he cautions: "But for some purposes it is useful to distinguish attitude from belief," and proceeds to refer to previous programs of prejudice reduction which have succeeded in altering beliefs but not in changing attitudes (the reverse of what the present findings indicate!). He continues: "Beliefs, to some extent can be rationally attacked and altered. Usually, however, they have the slippery propensity of accommodating themselves somehow to the negative attitude *which is much harder to change**. . . . Thus the belief system has a way of slithering around to justify the more permanent attitude system. The process is one of rationalization—of the accommodation of beliefs to attitudes." In the light of this position we shall in what follows refer to "attitudes of discrimination," as opposed to "prejudiced beliefs."

We now conclude that an indirect effect of the workshop was a significant relative decrease in *attitudes of discrimination*, as measured by the Bogardus scale. In addition we conclude that the indirect effects of the workshop do *not* include the significant relative decrease in prejudiced beliefs (noting, however, the relativity of the lack of significance).

* Author's underlining.

As we pause to consider the unexpectedly meaningful selectivity in the pattern of these results we are reminded of similar patternings in the detailed findings concerning self-acceptance. Briefly we recall that the experimental group has shown a significant increase in attitudes of self-acceptance and that this increase was primarily the result of a significant decrease in "projectivity," while "anti-intraception" remained largely unchanged. To this constellation of changes we may now add a significant decrease in attitudes of discrimination *and* (since for the moment we are considering the experimental group in isolation) in prejudiced beliefs. In contrast, we recall that the control groups showed a marked (at times significant) *decrease* in attitudes of self-acceptance, and that this decrease was primarily the result of a significant *increase* in anti-intraception, while projectivity remained largely unchanged. To *this* constellation of changes we may now add a decrease in prejudiced beliefs (not significant in itself but sufficient to make the corresponding decrease in the experimental group *relatively* insignificant) and *a negligible change in attitudes of discrimination*. These constellations of change are represented pictorially in Figure 1.

The unusual clarity in the patterning of the findings justifies speculation. This is best stated in a form pointed toward further research:

> *Hypothesis*: Both prejudiced beliefs *and* attitudes of discrimination can be indirectly reduced in association with the reduction of projective* tendencies.

> *Hypothesis*: Prejudiced beliefs can be reduced in association with *or in spite of* increased anti-intraceptive tendencies; attitudes of discrimination cannot.

Both hypotheses are supported by the evidence of this study but were not, of course, predicted.

Since attitudes of discrimination are presumably closely linked to a personality's action system and prejudiced beliefs to a personality's idea system we venture further into personality theory:

---

* We restrict this term to its defensive connotations in line with the term "projectivity."

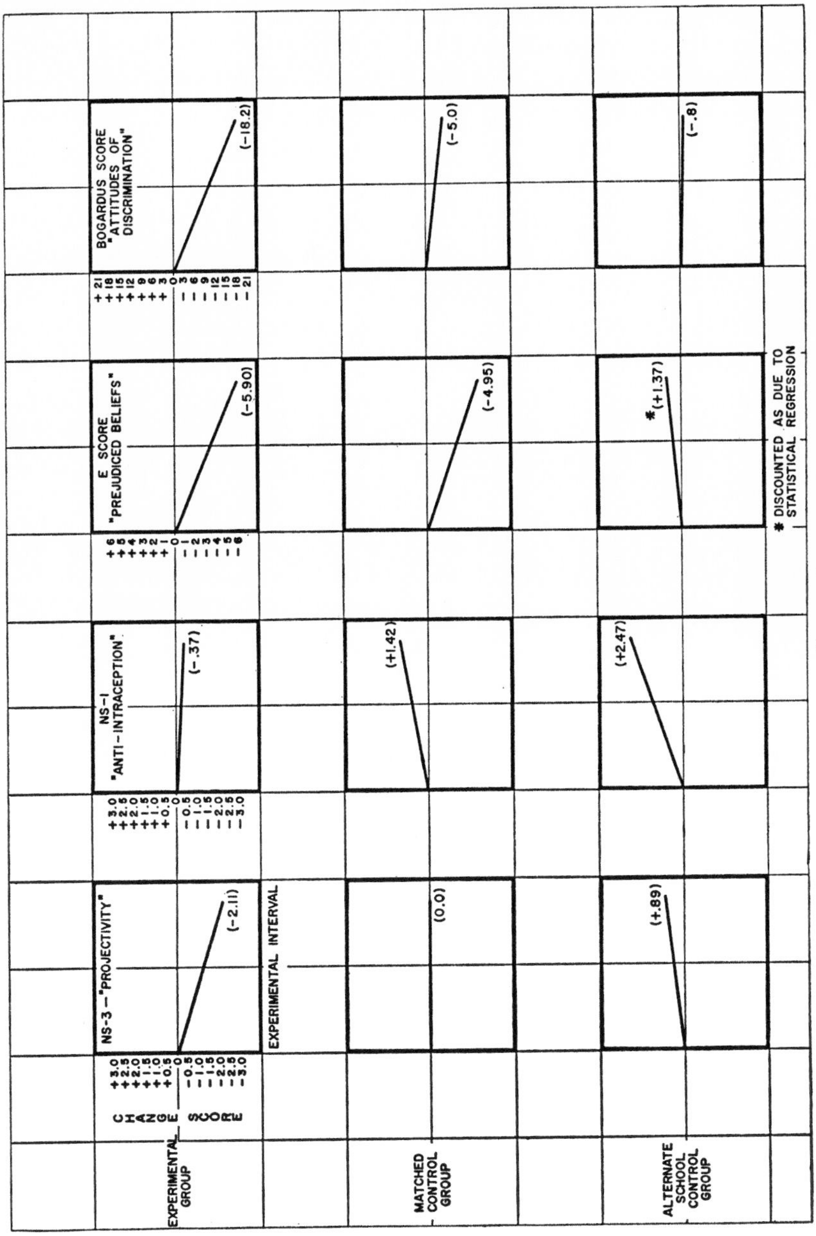
NS-3 — "PROJECTIVITY"
NS-I "ANTI-INTRACEPTION"
E SCORE "PREJUDICED BELIEFS"
BOGARDUS SCORE "ATTITUDES OF DISCRIMINATION"
CHANGE SCORE
EXPERIMENTAL GROUP
EXPERIMENTAL INTERVAL
MATCHED CONTROL GROUP
ALTERNATE SCHOOL CONTROL GROUP
(-2.11)
(-.37)
(-5.90)
(-18.2)
(0.0)
(+1.42)
(-4.95)
(-5.0)
(+.89)
(+2.47)
*(+1.37)
(-.8)
* DISCOUNTED AS DUE TO STATISTICAL REGRESSION

FIGURE 1

*Hypothesis*: Projectivity tends to be integrated in the organization of personality with the action system, i.e., in its defensive functions with "acting out."

*Hypothesis*: Anti-intraception tends to be integrated in the organization of personality with the idea system, i.e., in its defensive functions with "rationalization."

We pause to note that of the two systems, at least in their defensive functions, the projection-action system is the "deeper" of the two. We have reason to believe, for example, from much developmental research that "actions," recognizable as such, precede "ideas" (77). We also have reason to believe that projection precedes rationalization as a defense in the development of the ego (38). In the context of prejudice reduction we refer again to Allport's observations that one's beliefs are much more likely to accommodate "the more permanent" attitudes of discrimination than is the reverse to occur—thus accounting, for example, for the successful educational reduction of prejudiced beliefs, in the studies to which Allport refers, without a similar reduction in attitudes of discrimination.

If we assume the hypotheses stated above to be valid we are in a position to make an interesting speculative reconstruction of the actual experiences of the experimental and control groups.

The effect of the workshop was to free the experimental group to a significant degree from its defensive needs to project, thus indirectly reducing related *attitudes of discrimination*. The more readily influenced prejudiced beliefs may have been reduced, in the experimental group, either as a by-product of this more basic change or in relation to other ideological changes such as those represented in the TFI scale. In the control groups there were no such related positive ideological changes, and so we associate the singular reduction of prejudiced beliefs with the increase in anti-intraceptive tendencies.

The essence of anti-intraception ("only me") is conformity to the accepted norms of one's immediate environment—and it is here that we are startled into realizing *where* we are, so to say; namely, in a cultural center of New England, a major industry being higher education. In such a setting we know that verbalized prejudice is as unpopular as is verbalized tolerance in the deep south, and we recall that the sample populations had been drawn from a nationally representative population. Thus we account for the control group's decreased agreement with the prejudiced statements on the E scale by citing its increased (anti-intraceptive) needs to conform to the stereotyped (anti-prejudice) norms of the community in which it happened to be residing.

This assertion, of course, in no way excludes the possibility that the experimental group was similarly influenced by the attitudinal climate of the community. However, the evidence does exclude increased anti-intraception as a vehicle for this influence. On the other hand, the evidence strongly suggests that whatever influences were being exerted by the community were implemented in the experimental group and not in the control groups by on-going personality changes of sufficient depth to integrate reduced prejudiced beliefs *with* reduced attitudes of discrimination.

The previous reduction studies cited by Allport must often have asked: *How* can a belief be altered without effecting a corresponding alteration in related attitudes? To this question we suggest from this discussion: by offering one set of unintegrated beliefs for another, i.e., by offering anti-intolerance for intolerance. It is as if one's emotional needs for the *idea* of an outside something to be against do not quibble over the details—so long as it is *outside* (i.e., not me) and so long as one can continue to be *against* it.

We conclude that the increase in attitudes of self-acceptance, demonstrated to have been facilitated by the Self-Knowledge Workshop, has indirectly reduced to a significant degree both prejudiced beliefs and attitudes of discrimination, in addition to those social attitudes that perpetuate and sustain ethnic prejudice. We also conclude that these reductions were primarily implemented by reduced needs on the part of the workshop members to employ projective defenses.

The single appreciable change in the social attitudes of the control subjects involved reduced prejudiced beliefs. This change may have been caused by uncontrolled socio-cultural pressures toward "anti-intolerance," with the implementation of the increased anti-intraceptive tendencies shown to have been the effect of the experimental interval on the control subjects.

Finally, a note on the *magnitude* of the observed attitudinal changes is in order. The workshop worked no miracles. There were no neurotics cured, nor was anyone's future happiness assured. A measurably significant increase in attitudes of self-acceptance was observed, which, in the author's opinion, justified the investments made by the students and by the teacher; certainly the results justify such an enterprise as a worthwhile addition to a high school curriculum. Likewise, with respect to race prejudice: No bigots were transformed, and if the observed reduction in race prejudice were the lone result of the workshop it can hardly be said to have earned its keep. As an *indirect* effect of an otherwise demonstrably worthwhile enterprise, however, the reduction in race prejudice represents a real bonus.

# CRITERIA FOR RATING EGO THREATENING (ET) ITEMS

All ratings take into account the combined meaning of both stem and ending. Overall definition of an ego-threatening item:

Any item which states or strongly implies any attitude, feeling, or action that would be held in disapproval for a seventeen year old upper middle class girl according to the average social standards accruing to this segment of society (i.e., superego threat).

*or*

Any item which states or strongly implies any attitude, feeling, or action, which, if accepted by a seventeen year old upper middle class girl as applying to herself, would involve confronting at least a mild degree of psychological pain (i.e., ego threat).

The following sub-categories were used in order to achieve greater precision of scoring:

I. Socially disapproved behavior

*Examples*

1. When no one paid attention to me I—showed off.
2. When Jane's mother bothers her she—just shuts her ears.
3. If her brother loved a girl she disliked she would—probably be quite nasty.
4. When Jane was refused she—became sullen.
5. When she meets someone who is rich she—puts on an act.

II. Poorly controlled behavior

*Examples*

1. When her mother bothers her she—threw a tantrum.

2. When her father decides for her Jane—gets angry.
3. When complimented by the principal she—got flustered.
4. When she was accused she—began to cry.
5. When she is unsure she—gets nervous.

III. "Insightful" responses
—(Scorable only if "insight" is of at least a mildly "painful" nature, i.e., if it involves a "dropping of defenses.")
*Examples*

1. When they made fun of her she—just laughed *and cringed inside*.
2. When complimented by the principal she—withdrew and became painfully self-conscious.
3. When the talk is about boys Jane feels—rather uncomfortable.
4. When no one paid attention to me I—felt lost.
5. Most of all I fear—not being liked.

IV. Self-derogatory responses
—(must be socially disapproved or "painful" ones, i.e., not "properly self-effacing" or "modest" references)
*Examples*

1. I'm most ashamed of—my excess drinking.
2. She felt helpless when—he took her candy.
3. Jane was glad when—I left.
4. The supervisor makes Jane feel—like two cents.

V. Symbolically threatening responses
—(must be relatively undisguised)
*Examples*

1. She's most ashamed of—her scar.
2. She felt helpless when—the lights went out.
3. Most of all I fear—the dark.
4. Jane is most afraid of—bugs.
5. Jane is most afraid of—the bus that passes her house.

VI. Irrational responses
*Examples*

1. If Jane's father is wrong she—still thinks he's right.
2. When no one paid attention to me I—started to laugh.
3. When she meets someone who's rich she—shoots him.

VII. Thinly disguised forbidden wish responses

*Examples*

1. When she was neglected she—tried to be helpless.
2. When she meets someone who is rich she—immediately tears him down.
3. She felt helpless when—the car ran over her friend.

*Unscorable responses*

A response may be unscorable on the basis of:

1. Indecisiveness
2. Blandness
3. Ambiguity
4. Irrelevance
5. Lack of "threat"
6. Frequency

*Examples*

1. If Jane's brother or sister interferes she—has trouble controlling her temper.
2. I'm most ashamed of—my weaknesses.
3. She's most ashamed of—biting her fingernails.
4. When my mother bothers me I—leave the room.
5. When she got the prize she—cried.
6. Discussions about boys make me feel—frustrated.
7. I'm most ashamed of—my untidiness.
8. I felt helpless when—he asked me to aid.
9. She felt helpless when—she saw the child wavering on the tip of the rail.
10. When I was refused I—couldn't have felt more depressed.

## POST-WORKSHOP STATEMENTS IN ANSWER TO THE QUESTION: TO WHAT EXTENT DO YOU FEEL THAT THIS COURSE HAS DEALT WITH THE TOPIC OF RACE PREJUDICE?

1. I don't feel it has been dealt with.
2. I don't think this course has dealt with race prejudice at all—if it has dealt with prejudice it has been more in people's emotional and mental make-up, etc. than the externals of race.
3. The stereotype is the same but the realization that everyone has the same emotions at different stages has been discussed.
4. I don't think this course has dealt with race prejudice in any way.
5. I don't think this course has dealt with race prejudice at all.
6. Thinking about race prejudice I cannot remember much about the subject being brought up in the discussions.
7. I don't feel it has at all.
8. I don't think we have discussed too much about it—I cannot judge.
9. I don't think we have ever even discussed race prejudice.
10. Not at all to my knowledge.
11. I do not think this course dealt with race prejudice at all. Any ideas of race prejudice are probably already formed in an individual's mind before the course began.
12. I don't remember that we have ever even discussed race prejudice in class therefore I don't feel we have dealt with it to any extent at all.

13. I hadn't been under the impression that other than those isolated tests it was even mentioned.

14. I don't think that we have dealt with it at all or have found it a problem or subject. We have spoken in connection to L's relatives but I don't think any feeling against a particular race was aroused—only against a specific individual who we all recognize as apart from the race.

15. I don't believe that we have dealt hardly any at all in this field.

16. We may have talked about it in class once in a *great* while and it has been on a lot of the tests that we have had. I would say that we haven't done much with it as far as the course is concerned.

17. Not at all—in fact I can't remember the topic of race prejudice even coming up in the class or group meetings.

18. We've never brought up the subject, but if my memory is correct one time L. said something about her maid and she called her a "nigger"—this to my way of thinking was a symbol of her prejudice. We've never discussed this because we didn't feel a need for it.

19. None whatsoever—only in those tests.

# BIBLIOGRAPHY

1. Ackerman, N. and Jahoda, M.: *Anti-Semitism and Emotional Disorder*, New York: Harper and Brothers, 1950.
2. Adorno, Frenkel-Brunswick, Levinson, Sanford: *The Authoritarian Personality*, New York: Harper and Brothers, 1950.
3. Allport, G. W.: *The Nature of Prejudice*, Cambridge: Addison-Wesley Publishing Co., Inc., 1954.
4. Allport, G. W.: *Personality*, New York: Henry Holt and Company, 1937.
5. Allport, G. W.: *The Use of Personal Documents in Psychological Science*, Social Science Research Council, New York, 1942.
6. Allport, G. W.: *A Psychological Approach to the Study of Love and Hate*, Chapter 7 in P. A. Sorokin (Ed.) Explorations in Altruistic Love and Behavior, Boston: Beacon Press, 1950.
7. Allport, G. W.: *Catharsis and the Reduction of Prejudice*, Journal of Social Issues, 1945, 1, 3-10.
8. Allport, G. W.: *Basic Principals in Improving Human Relations*, Chapter 2 in K. W. Bigelow (Ed.), Cultural Groups and Human Relations, New York: Columbia Univ. Press, 1951.
9. Allport, G. W.: *The Resolution of Intergroup Tensions*, New York: National Conference of Christians and Jews, 1953.
10. Allport, G. W. and Kramer, B. M.: *Some Roots of Prejudice*, Journal of Psychology, 1946, 22, 9-39.
11. Asch, M. J.: *Nondirective Teaching in Psychology: An Experimental Study*, Psychological Monographs, 1951, Vol. 65, No. 4.
12. Ash, P. and Abramson, E.: *The Effect of Anonymity of Attitude-Questionnaire Response*, Journal of Abnormal and Social Psychology, 1952, 47, 722-723.
13. Berger, E. M.: *The Relation between Expressed Acceptance of Self and Expressed Acceptance of Others*, Journal of Abnormal and Social Psychology, 1952, 47, 778-782.

14. Berman, Leo: *Psychoanalysis and Group Psychotherapy*, The Psychoanalytic Review, 1950, 37, 2, 156-163.

15. Berman, Leo: *Mental Hygiene for Educators: Report on an Experiment Using a Combined Seminar and Group Psychotherapy Approach*, The Psychoanalytic Review, 1953, 40, 4, 319-332.

16. Berman, Leo: *A Group Psychotherapeutic Technique for Training in Clinical Psychology*, The American Journal of Orthopsychiatry, 1953, 23, 2, 322-327.

17. Bettelheim, B. and Janowitz, M.: *Dynamics of Prejudice*, New York: Harper and Brothers, 1950.

18. Bogardus, E. H.: *A Social Distance Scale*, Sociology and Social Research, 1933, 17, 265-271.

19. Bogardus, E. H.: *The Intercultural Workshop and Racial Distance*, Sociology and Social Research, 1948, 32, 798-802.

20. Bruner, J.: *Social Psychology*, Annual Review of Psychology, 1950, Vol. 1, 120.

21. Bullis, H. E.: *An Educational Program for the Development of the Normal Personality*, American Journal of Psychiatry, 1952, 109, 375-377.

22. Chance, E.: *A Study of Transference in Group Psychotherapy*, International Journal of Group Psychotherapy, 1952, 2, 40-53.

23. Coffey, H., Freedman, M., Leary, T., Ossorio, A.: *Group Psychotherapy in a Church Program*, The Journal of Social Issues, 1950, Vol. 6, No. 1.

24. Cronbach, L. J.: *Educational Psychology*, Annual Review of Psychology, 1950, Vol. 1, 238-239.

25. Crutchfield: *Social Psychology*, Annual Review of Psychology, 1954, Vol. 5

26. Davis, A.: *The Ego and Status-Anxiety*, The State of the Social Sciences, L. D. White, Editor, Univ. of Chicago Press, 1956.

27. Dorris, R. J., Levinson, D. J. and Hanfmann, E.: *Authoritarian Personality Studied by a New Variation of the Sentence Completion Technique*, Journal of Abnormal and Social Psychology, 1954, 49, 1, 99-108.

28. Dorsey, J. M.: *A Psychotherapeutic Approach to the Problem of of Hostility*, Social Forces, 1950, 29, 2, 197-206.

29. Driver, H. I.: *Multiple Counseling*, Madison, Wisc.: Monona Publications, 1954.

30. Erikson, E. H.: *Childhood and Society*, New York: Norton, 1950.

31. Erikson, E. H.: *Growth and Crises of the 'Healthy Personality,'* Personality, Kluckhohn, Murray and Schneider, Chapter 12, New York: Knopf, 1953.

32. Fenichel, O.: *The Psycho-Analysis of Anti-Semitism,* American Imago, 1, 1940, 24-39.

33. Frank, L. K.: *Newer Approaches to Sex Education,* Pastoral Psychology, 1951, 1, 10, 19-24.

34. Frank, L. K.: *This is the Adolescent,* Understanding the Child, 1949, 18, 65-69.

35. Frenkel-Brunswick, E.: *A Study of Prejudice in Children,* Human Relations, 1949, 1, 295-306.

36. Frenkel-Brunswick, E.: *Mechanisms of Self Deception,* Journal of Social Psychology, 1939, 10, 409-420.

37. Frenkel-Brunswick, E. and Sanford, R. N.: *Some Personality Correlates of Anti-Semitism,* Journal of Psychology, 1945, 20, 271-291.

38. Freud, A.: *Ego and Mechanisms of Defense,* New York: International Universities Press, 1946.

39. Freud, S.: *The Passing of the Oedipus Complex.* In Collected Papers, Vol. 2, London: Hogarth Press, 1943.

40. Freud, S.: *The Infantile Genital Organization of the Libido.* In Collected Papers, Vol. 2, London: Hogarth Press, 1943.

41. Freud, S.: *On the Sexual Theories of Children.* In Collected Papers, Vol. 2, London: Hogarth Press, 1943.

42. Freud, S.: *Infantile Mental Life.* In Collected Papers, Vol. 2, London: Hogarth Press, 1943.

43. Gardner, G. E.: *Security and Adjustment,* Mental Hygiene, 1951, 35, 353-364.

44. Getzels, J. W.: *The Assessment of Personality and Prejudice by the Method of Paired Direct and Projective Questionnaires,* Doctoral Dissertation, Harvard University, 1951.

45. Hanfmann, E.: *William Stern on Projective Techniques,* Journal of Personality, 1953, 21, 1-21.

46. Hanfmann, E. and Getzels, J. W.: *Studies of the Sentence Completion Test,* Journal of Projective Techniques, 1953, 17, 3, 280-294.

47. Haimowitz, M. L. and Haimowitz, N. R.: *Reducing Ethnic Hostility through Psychotherapy,* Journal of Social Psychology, 1950, 31, 231-241.

48. Jahoda, M. and West, P. E.: *Race Relations in Public Housing,* Journal of Social Issues, 1951, 7, 132-139.

49. Jahoda, M., Deutsch, M. and Cook, S. W.: *Research Methods in Social Relations: With Special Reference to Prejudice*, New York: Dryden Press, 1951.

50. Jershild, A. T.: *In Search of Self*, New York: Teachers College, Columbia Univ., 1952.

51. Josselyn, I. M.: *The Adolescent and His World*, New York: Family Service Association of America, 1952.

52. Josselyn, I. M.: *Psychological Problems of the Adolescent*, Social Casework, 1951, 32, 183-190 and 250-254.

53. Kagan, H. E.: *Changing the Attitudes of Christian toward Jew*, New York: Columbia Univ. Press, 1952.

54. Kris, E.: *On Psychoanalysis and Education*, American Journal of Orthopsychiatry, 1948, 18, 4.

55. Kubie, L. S.: *The Forgotten Man of Education*, Harvard Alumni Bulletin, 1954, Feb. 6.

56. Kubie, L. S.: *A Research Project in Community Mental Hygiene: A Fantasy*, Mental Hygiene, 1952, 36, 220-226.

57. Kubie, L. S.: Unpublished notes.

58. Kutner, B. J.: *Patterns of Mental Functioning Associated with Prejudice in Children* (Unpublished), Cambridge: Harvard College Library, 1950.

59. Langer, S.: *Philosophy in a New Key*, New York: Mentor, 1942.

60. Levinson, D. J.: *The Intergroup Relations Workshop: Its Psychological Aims and Effects*, Journal of Psychology, 1954, 38, 103-126.

61. Levinson, D. J. and Sanford, R. N.: *A Scale for the Measurement of Anti-Semitism*, Journal of Psychology, 1944, 17, 339-370.

62. Lewin, K.: *Resolving Social Conflicts*, New York: Harper and Brothers, 1948.

63. Lindzey, G.: *Differences Between the High and Low in Prejudice and Their Implications for a Theory of Prejudice*, Journal of Personality, 1950, 19, 16-40.

64. Maas, H. S.: *Applying Group Therapy to Classroom Practice*, Mental Hygiene, 1951, 35, 2, 250-259.

65. Maccay, E.: Unpublished notes.

66. Maslow, A. H.: *Self Actualizing People: A study of psychological health*, Personality, 1950, Symposium No. 1, 11-34.

67. Maslow, A. H.: *The Authoritarian Character Structure*, Journal of Social Psychology, 1943, 18, 401-411.

68. May, R.: *Man's Search for Himself*, New York; Norton and Co., 1953.

69. McNassor, D.: *Conflict in Teachers Who Try to Learn About Children*, California Journal of Educational Research, 1951, Sept., 147-155.

70. Moreno, J. L.: *Psychodrama*, New York: Beacon House, 1946.

71. Mosteller, R. and Bush, R. R.: *Selected Quantitative Techniques*, Chapter 8, Handbook of Social Psychology, edited by Gardner Lindzey, Cambridge: Addison-Wesley, 1954.

72. Murray, H. A.: Unpublished notes.

73. Mussen, P. H.: *Factors Changing Children's Attitudes Toward Negroes*, Journal of Abnormal and Social Psychology, 1950, 45, 423-441.

74. Newcomb, T. M.: *Social Psychology*, New York: Dryden Press, 1950.

75. Pearl, D.: *Ethnocentrism and the Concept of the Self*, Ph.D. dissertation, Univ. of Chicago, 1950.

76. Piaget, J.: *Play, Dreams and Imitation in Childhood*, New York: Norton, 1951.

77. Rapaport, D.: *Organization and Pathology of Thought*, New York: Columbia Univ. Press, 1951.

78. Rieken, H. W.: *The Volunteer Workcamp: A Psychological Evaluation*, Cambridge: Addison-Wesley, 1952.

79. Rogers, C. R. and Dymond, R. F.: *Psychotherapy and Personality Change*, Univ. of Chicago Press, 1954.

80. Rogers, C. R.: *Client-Centered Therapy*, Boston: Houghton-Mifflin Co., 1951.

81. Rokeach, M.: *Generalized Mental Rigidity as a Factor in Ethnocentrism*, Journal of Abnormal and Social Psychology, 1948, 43, 259-278.

82. Rosenthal, S.: *A Fifth Grade Classroom Experiment in Fostering Mental Health*, Journal of Child Psychiatry, Vol. 2, Sec. 3.

83. Saenger, G. and Gilbert, E.: *Customer Reactions to the Integration of Negro Sales Personnel*, International Journal of Opinion and Attitude Research, 1950, 4, 57-76.

84. Schactel, E. G.: *On Memory and Childhood Amnesia*, Psychiatry, 1947, 10, 1, 1-26.

85. Scodel, A. and Mussen, P.: *Social Perceptions of Authoritarians and Non-Authoritarians*, Journal of Abnormal and Social Psychology, 1953, 48, 181-184.

86. Seeley, J. R.: *The Forest Hill Village Project: An Action Research.* Unpublished.

87. Semrad, E. V.: Personal communication.
88. Sheerer, E. T.: *An Analysis of the Relationship between Acceptance of and Respect for Self and Acceptance of and Respect for Others in Ten Counseling Cases*, Journal of Consulting Psychology, 1949, 13, 169-175.
89. Silberer, H.: *On Symbol-Formation*, in Rapaport, op. cit., 208-234.
90. Slavson, S. R.: *Creative Group Education*, New York: Association Press, 1948.
91. Solomon, R. L.: *An Extension of the Control Group Design*, Psychological Bulletin, 1949, 46, 137-150.
92. Stock, D.: *An Investigation into the Interrelations between the Self Concept and Feelings Directed toward Other Persons and Groups*, Journal of Consulting Psychology, 1949, 13, 3, 176-180.
93. Stoufer, S. A., et al.: *The American Soldier*, Princeton University Press, 1949, Vol. 2.
94. Strang, R.: *Counseling Technics in College and Secondary School*, New York: Harper and Brothers, 1949.
95. Sullivan, H. S.: *Conceptions of Modern Psychiatry*, William Allen White Psychiatric Foundation, Washington, 1947.
96. Toman, W.: *Zum Problem der Psychoanalytischen Theorie*, Studuim Generale, Springer, Heidelberg, 1953.
97. Weinreb, J.: *Report of an Experience in the Application of Dynamic Psychiatry in Education*, Mental Hygiene, 1953, 37, 2, 283-293.
98. Whitehead, A. N.: *The Aims of Education*, New York: Mentor, 1949.
99. Wieder, G. S.: *Group Procedures Modifying Attitudes of Prejudice in the College Classroom*, Journal of Educational Psychology, 1954, 45, 6, 332-344.

# INDEX